Econometrics - Recent Advances and Applications

Edited by Brian W. Sloboda

Published in London, United Kingdom

Econometrics - Recent Advances and Applications
http://dx.doi.org/10.5772/intechopen.100862
Edited by Brian W. Sloboda

Contributors
Yixiao Jiang, Oral Capps, Lijia Mo, Thobeka Ncanywa, Noko Setati, Jonathan Lee, Alex Lenkoski, Bjørnar Karlsen Kivedal

First published in London, United Kingdom, 2023 by IntechOpen
IntechOpen is the global imprint of INTECHOPEN LIMITED, registered in England and Wales, registration number: 11086078, 5 Princes Gate Court, London, SW7 2QJ, United Kingdom
Printed in Croatia

British Library Cataloguing-in-Publication Data
A catalogue record for this book is available from the British Library

Additional hard and PDF copies can be obtained from orders@intechopen.com

Econometrics - Recent Advances and Applications
Edited by Brian W. Sloboda
p. cm.

This title is part of the Business, Management and Economics Book Series, Volume 10
Topic: Economics
Series Editor: Taufiq Choudhry
Topic Editor: Jaime Ortiz

Print ISBN 978-1-80356-524-8
Online ISBN 978-1-80356-525-5
eBook (PDF) ISBN 978-1-80356-526-2
ISSN 2753-894X

For EU product safety concerns:
IN TECH d.o.o., Prolaz Marije Krucifikse Kozulić 3, 51000 Rijeka, Croatia,
info@intechopen.com or visit our website at intechopen.com.

IntechOpen Book Series

Business, Management and Economics

Volume 10

Aims and Scope of the Series

This series will provide a comprehensive overview of recent research trends in business and management, economics, and marketing. Topics will include asset liability management, financial consequences of the financial crisis and covid-19, financial accounting, mergers and acquisitions, management accounting, SMEs, financial markets, corporate finance and governance, managerial technology and innovation, resource management and sustainable development, social entrepreneurship, corporate responsibility, ethics and accountability, microeconomics, labour economics, macroeconomics, public economics, financial economics, econometrics, direct marketing, creative marketing, internet marketing, market planning and forecasting, brand management, market segmentation and targeting and other topics under business and management. This book series will focus on various aspects of business and management whose in-depth understanding is critical for business and company management to function effectively during this uncertain time of financial crisis, Covid-19 pandemic, and military activity in Europe.

Meet the Series Editor

Prof. Choudhry holds a BSc degree in Economics from the University of Iowa, as well as a Masters and Ph.D. in Applied Economics from Clemson University, USA. In January 2006, he became a Professor of Finance at the University of Southampton Business School. He was previously a Professor of Finance at the University of Bradford Management School. He has over 80 articles published in international finance and economics journals. His research interests and specialties include financial econometrics, financial economics, international economics and finance, housing markets, financial markets, among others.

Meet the Volume Editor

Brian W. Sloboda is an economist at the US Department of Labor and a faculty member at the University of Maryland, Global Campus where he teaches economics and finance. His research focuses on regional economics, economic growth, and labor economics with avocational research interests in finance and presidential election forecasting models. He is a committee member of the Federal Forecasters Consortium (FFC), a board member of the Pennsylvania Economics Association, and a member of the editorial board of *Pennsylvania Economic Review*. Dr. Sloboda is the former president of the Society of Government Economists (SGE) and is now its executive director. He is currently an assistant editor for the *Journal of Economics* and a senior social science editor for the *European Scientific Journal*. He is also a book review editor for the *Review of Regional Studies*.

Contents

Preface

Econometric analysis forms the basis of empirical economic research. Our education taught us that econometrics is more than compiling data and running an ordinary least squares (OLS) regression to answer a research question(s). Specifically, econometrics helps us identify good ideas from bad ones and assesses research questions. Econometrics is applied economics that enables us to see the complicated world and assess the relationships in which policymakers and analysts could prescribe policy. *Econometrics – Recent Advances and Applications* uses applied econometric methods to answer interesting research questions. It includes six chapters written by experts in economics and finance. The book addresses the application of econometric methods to various fields in economics. As such, it is a useful resource for academicians, researchers, and practitioners in economics and finance.

The chapters in this book provide a theoretical framework for applying econometrics to a particular problem. In empirical research, the acquisition of the appropriate data is paramount. The chapters not only present applications of econometric methods but also provide unique datasets that can be used in empirical research.

Chapter 1, "Evaluating DSGE Models: From Calibration to Cointegration" by Bjørnar Karlsen Kivedal, examines the historical development of estimating new Keynesian dynamic stochastic equilibrium (DSGE) models. The author focuses on how cointegration can be used to test and estimate the relationships in these models. An empirical assessment of a model is crucial to validate the theory, and this should be an important step when analyzing DSGE models. The author illustrates different techniques for estimating DSGE models and compares these methods to using cointegration when estimating and evaluating DSGE models.

Chapter 2, "A Primer on Machine Learning Methods for Credit Rating Modeling" by Yixiao Jiang, studies the important features of predicting corporate bond ratings. There is a growing literature on predicting credit ratings via machine learning methods. However, there have been fewer empirical studies using ensemble methods, which refer to the technique of combining the prediction of multiple classifiers. This chapter compares six machine learning models: ordered logit model (OL), neural network (NN), support vector machine (SVM), bagged decision trees (BDTs), random forest (RF), and gradient-boosted machines (GBMs). This chapter may also serve as a primer for empirical researchers who want to learn machine learning methods by providing an intuitive description of each employed method. The author employed Moody's ratings using data collected from 2001 to 2017. Three broad categories of features, including financial ratios, equity risk, and bond issuer's cross-ownership relation with the credit rating agencies, were explored in the modeling phase, using the data before 2016. These models were tested in an evaluation phase, using the most recent data after 2016.

In Chapter 3, "Forecasting Weekly Shipments of Hass Avocados from Mexico to the United States Using Econometric and Vector Autoregression Models", Oral Capps discusses how domestic production cannot meet the US demand for avocados, satisfying only 10% of the national demand. Due to year-round production and longer shelf life, the Hass variety of avocados account for about 85% of avocados consumed in the United States and roughly 95% of total avocado imports, primarily from Mexico. Using weekly data from July 3, 2011, to October 24, 2021, the author estimated econometric and vector autoregression models regarding the seven main shipment sizes of Hass avocados from Mexico to the United States. Both models discern the impacts of inflation-adjusted and exchange-rate-adjusted prices per box, US disposable income, holidays, and events, and seasonality on the level of Hass avocado shipments by size. These impacts are generally robust across the respective models by shipment size. These models also mimic the variability in the level of shipments by size quite well based on goodness-of-fit metrics. Based on absolute percent error, these models provide reasonably accurate forecasts of Hass avocado shipments from Mexico by size associated with a time horizon of 13 weeks. However, neither type of model provides a better forecast performance universally across all avocado shipment sizes.

Chapter 4, "Spatiotemporal Difference-in-Differences: A Dynamic Mechanism of Socio-Economic Evaluation" by Lijia Mo delves into spatial econometrics, an expanding area in econometrics. Advances in econometric modeling and analysis of spatial cross-sectional and spatial panel data assist in revealing the spatiotemporal characteristics behind socioeconomic phenomena and improving prediction accuracy. Difference-in-differences (DID) is frequently used in causality inference and estimation of the treatment effect of the policy intervention in different time and space dimensions. Relying on flexible distributional hypotheses of treatment versus experiment groups on spillover, spatiotemporal DID provides space for innovation and alternatives, taking spatial heterogeneity, dependence, and proximity into consideration. This chapter gives a practical econometric evaluation of the dynamic mechanism in this spatiotemporal context and a toolkit for this fulfillment.

Chapter 5, "The Impact of Inflation Expectations and Public Debt on Taxation in South Africa" by Thobeka Ncanywa and Noko Setati, investigates the impact of inflation expectations and public debt on taxation in South Africa, employing the autoregressive distributive lag model and Granger Causality techniques. The results indicate a long-term positive relationship between inflation expectations and taxation and a significant negative relationship between public debt and taxation. The empirical results reveal that taxable income will also increase when consumers and businesses expect the inflation rate to rise. The public debt–taxation nexus can imply that the South African government finances its debts through borrowing rather than through taxation. Therefore, economic participants must have full knowledge of what can influence taxation.

Finally, Chapter 6, "Incorporating Model Uncertainty in Market Response Models with Multiple Endogenous Variables by Bayesian Model Averaging" by Jonathan Lee and Alex Lenkoski, develops a method to incorporate model uncertainty by model averaging in generalized linear models subject to multiple endogeneity and instrumentation. Their approach builds on a Gibbs sampler for the instrumental variable framework that incorporates model uncertainty in both outcome and instrumentation stages. Direct evaluation of model probabilities is intractable in this setting. However, the authors show that by nesting model moves inside the Gibbs sampler, a model comparison can be performed via conditional Bayes factors, leading to straightforward calculations. This new Gibbs sampler is slightly more involved than the original algorithm and exhibits no evidence of mixing difficulties. They further show how the same principle may be employed to evaluate the validity of instrumentation choices. The authors conclude with an empirical marketing study of estimating opening box office by three endogenous regressors (prerelease advertising, opening screens, and production budget).

While *Econometrics – Recent Advances and Applications* covers many econometric methods, it is not an exhaustive presentation. Specifically, each of the chapters clearly outlines the research development starting with its research question(s), providing specific data sources that can be used, and outlining the econometric method used. The authors ably explain their empirical results and their meaning, which can be used in policy-making and other decisional cases. More importantly, carefully explaining the empirical results is an important craft and will be a good education for all readers, whether they are junior investigators or more advanced researchers refreshing their knowledge of methods and research. However, readers of *Econometrics – Recent Advances and Applications* should be familiar with research design as well as econometric methods (e.g., Stock and Watson (2019) and Wooldridge (2019)) to apply these methods appropriately.

Brian W. Sloboda
University of Maryland, Global Campus,
Aldelphi, Maryland, USA

Chapter 1

Evaluating DSGE Models: From Calibration to Cointegration

Bjørnar Karlsen Kivedal

Abstract

This chapter examines the historical development of estimating new Keynesian dynamic stochastic equilibrium (DSGE) models. I focus, in particular, on how cointegration can be used in order to test and estimate the relationships in these models using a simple RBC model as an example. Empirical evaluation of a model is critical to validate the theory, and this should be an essential step when analyzing DSGE models. The chapter illustrates the use of various estimation techniques when estimating DSGE models and compares these methods to using cointegration when estimating and evaluating DSGE models.

Keywords: DSGE models, calibration, estimation, cointegration, RBC model

1. Introduction

Some of the first aggregate macroeconometric models describing national business cycles were developed by Jan Tinbergen in the 1930s. A model for the US was published in 1939 [1], estimated recursively by the ordinary least squares method, based on theoretical dynamic business cycle models such as the one developed by [2]. Tinbergen's work was further developed by [3], who discussed testing economic theory by statistical inference using empirical observations. Furthermore, [4] emphasized using a system of simultaneous equations in order to model the economy and suggested using other estimation methods than ordinary least squares on each equation. Several macroeconometric models were constructed for the US following this, most notably from the work by the Cowles Commission for Research in Economics such as the models by [5, 6]. These were followed by a number of other models of the same type. See, for example, [7] for an historical overview of macroeconometric models.

Macroeconometric models such as these were constructed based on historical data, which was used both for estimating the parameters and for the model structure. A structural change in the economy could, therefore, lead to the econometric model not being relevant any more. If these models were not invariant to such changes, they would not be usable for policy analysis, as pointed out by [8]. This became known as "the Lucas critique," suggesting that the behavior of the agents in the economy needed to be explained by a structural model instead of aggregate historical relationships. This was needed in order to have a model invariant to policy changes.

Particularly, the parameters of the model, which determines tastes and preferences should be invariant to policy changes, while the remaining parts of the model should be regarded as stochastic.

In response to the Lucas critique, real business cycle (RBC) models, as introduced by [9], used microeconomic foundations, where consumers and firms optimized their intertemporal utility or profits using rational expectations. Extensions of the model with various rigidities, monopolistic competition, and short-run non-neutrality of monetary policy led to new Keynesian models,[1] which later has become the standard both for forecasting and policy evaluation (See e.g. [10]). These models are examples of dynamic stochastic general equilibrium (DSGE) models, and they are typically solved by finding the first-order conditions for the optimization problems of the representative agents of the model. The first-order conditions are then expressed in log deviation from the steady state of the model such that a (log) linear model is obtained. This yields a model where the variables are expressed as log deviations from their representative steady-state values, that is. approximating percentage deviation from steady state. Furthermore, the part of the model based on preferences should be invariant to policy changes since policy changes should be modeled as stochastic. Hence, the structural DSGE model may be tested by imposing the hypotheses from the model as restrictions on a statistical model. This amounts to testing the Lucas critique since the structural part of the model is tested. If it is not rejected, the model may be useful for policy analysis. DSGE models are often used for analyzing monetary policy. Among the most popular models used are the medium scale models in [11, 12], focusing on the US and the Euro area, respectively.

The RBC model of [9] can be considered a cornerstone of DSGE models, and DSGE models are typically extended versions of RBC models. RBC models include optimizing agents with rational expectations, and only one shock is sufficient to generate business cycles. This shock is usually a shock to technology or productivity and modeled as an exogenous variable that enters the production function. In addition to this, DSGE models also include frictions, which take a lot of observed dynamics into account. Most importantly are price stickiness, usually modeled as Calvo pricing [13]. Other frictions, such as wage rigidities (see [14, 15]), are also often found in DSGE models. Other shocks and rigidities are also often included in models in order to allow for more detailed dynamics. However, many of these frictions can be found relatively unimportant empirically, see [11], and thus not necessary to explain the dynamics found in the data.

In general, a nonlinear DSGE model can be formulated as

$$E_t\left[f\left(y_{t+1}, y_t, y_{t-1}, u_t\right)\right] = 0 \tag{1}$$

and has a rational expectations solution

$$y_t = g\left(y_{t-1}, u_t\right). \tag{2}$$

A linear approximation of such as model is usually used. This is given as

$$\hat{y}_t = T(\theta)\hat{y}_{t-1} + R(\theta)u_t, \tag{3}$$

[1] Although they were developed simultaneously as RBC models.

where T and R are time-invariant (which means that they depend on the structural parameters of the model) and $u_t \sim N(0, Q).\hat{y}_t = \log(y_t/\bar{y})$. This is then solved for the representative agent with full information about the model and the structural shocks. For more details, see, for example [16], which a lot of the presentation in this chapter is inspired by. Other useful sources for more information are [17–19].

The next section presents a simple RBC model, which is a special case of a DSGE model. The following sections use this model as an example in order to illustrate calibration, generalized method of moments, full information maximum likelihood, and Bayesian methods. Section 7 presents the cointegrated vector autoregressive model and how to test implications of a DSGE model, while the final section concludes. There is also some code relevant for investigating the model shown in Appendix A.

2. A simple RBC model

If we consider the simple RBC model in [20], we have households that maximize

$$E_t \sum_{t=0}^{\infty} \beta^t (\ln c_t + \gamma(1 - n_t)) \tag{4}$$

subject to the budget constraint

$$x_t + c_t = w_t n_t + r_t k_t \tag{5}$$

and

$$k_{t+1} = (1 - \delta)k_t + x_t. \tag{6}$$

Here, c_t is consumption and n_t labor (hours worked) in time t. γ is the utility weight, x_t investment, w_t real wage, r_t rental rate of capital, k_t capital stock, and δ the depreciation rate.

This yields the first-order conditions

$$1/c_t = \beta E_t((1/c_{t+1})(1 + r_{t+1} - \delta)) \tag{7}$$

$$\gamma c_t = w_t, \tag{8}$$

which provides the optimal choice of c_t, n_t and k_{t+1}. Eq. (7) is an Euler equation, while eq. (8) is the marginal rate of substitution.

A single good is produced by perfectly competitive firms (who maximize their profits each period)

$$y_t = z_t(k_t)^{\alpha}(n_t)^{1-\alpha}, \tag{9}$$

where $0 < \alpha < 1, y_t$ is output and z_t is the technology shock. The technology shock follows an exogenous stochastic process

$$\ln z_{t+1} = \rho \ln z_t + \varepsilon_{t+1}, \tag{10}$$

where ε_t is independently, identically, and normally distributed with zero mean and variance σ^2.

The firm chooses the input levels (capital and labor) to maximize profits, and the marginal product of labor (capital) equals the marginal product of the real wage (rental rate).

Hence, the competitive equilibrium is the sequence of prices $\{w_t, r_t\}_{t=0}^{\infty}$ and allocations $\{c_t, n_t, x_t, k_{t+1}, y_t\}_{t=0}^{\infty}$ such that firms maximize profits, agents maximize utility, and all markets clear. The structural parameters of the model are, thus, $\beta, \gamma, \delta, \alpha$ and ρ. These parameters describe behavior, and we are, therefore, interested in assessing the value of these parameters.

Some steady-state relationships of the model are

$$\frac{k}{n} = ((1/\beta + \delta - 1)/\alpha)^{1/(\alpha-1)} \tag{11}$$

$$\frac{c}{y} = 1 - \frac{\alpha(\beta + \delta - 1)}{\delta}. \tag{12}$$

Hence, the long-run relationship between capital and hours worked, k/n, and the long-run relationship between consumption and output, c/y, may be described by a combination of structural parameters and should, thus, be constant in the long run.

Such a model is often log-linearized (i.e. written in terms of log deviation from the theoretical steady state; $\hat{x}_t \equiv \log x_t - \log x$) in order to have a stationary representation. This yields,

$$\begin{aligned}
E_t\hat{c}_{t+1} &= \hat{c}_t + \alpha\beta(k/n)^{\alpha-1}\left[(\alpha-1)E_t\hat{k}_{t+1} + (1-\alpha)E_t\hat{n}_{t+1} + E_t\hat{z}_{t+1}\right] \\
\hat{n}_t &= -(1/\alpha)\hat{c}_t + \hat{k}_t + (1/\alpha)\hat{z}_t \\
\hat{y}_t &= \alpha\hat{k}_t + (1-\alpha)\hat{n}_t + \hat{z}_t \\
\hat{y}_t &= (1-\delta)(k/n)^{1-\alpha}\hat{c}_t + \left(1-(1-\delta)(k/n)^{1-\alpha}\right)\hat{x}_t \\
\hat{k}_{t+1} &= (1-\delta)\hat{k}_t + \delta\hat{x}_t \\
\hat{z}_{t+1} &= \rho\hat{z}_t + \varepsilon_t
\end{aligned} \tag{13}$$

where the log deviations can be interpreted as percentage deviations from the steady state.

The log-linearized model has the solution

$$\begin{aligned}
s_t &= \Phi\xi_t \\
\xi_t &= D\xi_{t-1} + v_t.
\end{aligned} \tag{14}$$

or

$$\begin{aligned}
\begin{bmatrix} \hat{y}_t \\ \hat{n}_t \\ \hat{c}_t \end{bmatrix} &= \begin{bmatrix} \phi_{yk} & \phi_{yz} \\ \phi_{nk} & \phi_{nz} \\ \phi_{ck} & \phi_{cz} \end{bmatrix} \begin{bmatrix} \hat{k}_t \\ \hat{z}_t \end{bmatrix} \\
\begin{bmatrix} \hat{k}_t \\ \hat{z}_t \end{bmatrix} &= \begin{bmatrix} d_{11} & d_{12} \\ d_{21} & d_{22} \end{bmatrix} \begin{bmatrix} \hat{k}_{t-1} \\ \hat{z}_{t-1} \end{bmatrix} + \begin{bmatrix} \varepsilon_t^k \\ \varepsilon_t^z \end{bmatrix}.
\end{aligned} \tag{15}$$

The eigenvalues and eigenvectors of the matrix in the system with expectational terms are used in order to calculate the Φ matrix.

There are different ways of obtaining values for the parameters $\{\beta, \gamma, \delta, \alpha, \rho\}$ in the model. Using calibration, we choose the values subjectively or objectively in order to use the model for simulation, while we may estimate the value of the parameters based on observed economic data $\{c_t, n_t, y_t\}_{t=0}^{T}$ by using statistical methods. In the next sections, we will compare calibration and estimation using generalized method of moments (GMM), full information maximum likelihood (FIML), Bayesian methods, and the cointegrated vector autoregressive (CVAR) model.

3. Calibration

At first, these models were mainly calibrated and simulated, as proposed by [9]. This was done by fixing the values of structural parameters according to empirical studies in microeconomics or moments of the data such as long-run "great ratios" representing historical relationships between the variables.

We can calibrate the RBC model in [20], by setting the parameter values of the model, that is. assigning values to $\{\beta, \gamma, \delta, \alpha, \rho\}$. This was popular before one was technically able to estimate large models and used in order to undertake computational experiments with the model. Hence, it is not possible to estimate parameters and test hypotheses regarding these when using calibration.

Calibration is, often, used in order to back out shocks (shock decomposition) and compares correlations between simulated variables and the data. Outcomes of the calibrated model may then be compared to descriptive statistics (e.g. the moments) of the data, and the model may be used in order to forecast or conduct policy analysis. The in-sample forecast performance may be assessed using measures such as root mean squared errors.

Hence, it is possible to do judgments of how the model fits the empirical reality even if we do not estimate the model. Calibration may also be useful as a first impression of the model before it is completely developed and estimated. However, we are not able to say anything about uncertainty. It may also be a useful approach when data are not available or only small samples can be obtained, which can be relevant for some regions and countries.

4. Generalized method of moments

Later, estimation using generalized method of moments (GMM) for single equations was conducted in order to estimate some of the parameters in the model. See, for example, [21] or [22] for estimation of the new Keynesian Phillips curve. GMM was introduced by [23] and first applied to DSGE models by [24, 25].

The method consists of minimizing the distance between some functions of the data and the model. Estimation can, therefore, be conducted using the (nonlinear) first-order conditions such that it is not required that we solve the model before estimating the parameters. However, we need a set of moment conditions in order to perform GMM, and it is a type of limited information estimation since we only utilize part of the theoretical model and not necessarily observations for all of the variables in the model. In particular, we have no likelihood function but only specific moments of interest that are adjusted to the data (called matching moments or orthogonality conditions).

Hence, we aim to minimize the distance between the observed moments from the sample and the population moments as implied by the model. In general, we have that the estimate of a parameter θ (is)

$$\hat{\theta}_T = \arg\min_{\theta} Q_T(\theta) \tag{16}$$

where

$$Q_T = \frac{1}{T}\sum_{t-1}^{T} f(y_t, \theta)' W_T \frac{1}{T}\sum_{t-1}^{T} f(y_t, \theta). \tag{17}$$

Here, W_T is the weighting matrix, which is used if there are more moment conditions than parameters. We, thus, seek to minimize Q_T, which is the square product of the sample moment, by the value of θ. The GMM estimator of θ is, thus, the value of θ that minimizes Q_T.

We may consider the Euler equation in the RBC model in [20], which was

$$1/c_t = \beta E_t((1/c_{t+1})(1 + r_{t+1} - \delta)). \tag{18}$$

In order to estimate the parameters $\{\beta, \delta\}$, we have two conditions since there are two parameters in one condition (equation). The first moment condition can be the Euler equation

$$E_t\left[\beta \frac{c_{t+1}}{c_t}(1 + r_{t+1} - \delta)\right] = 0, \tag{19}$$

or more correctly that $E_t\left[\beta \frac{c_{t+1}}{c_t}(1 + r_{t+1} - \delta)\right] \cdot 1 = 0$. The second may be

$$E_t\left[\beta \frac{c_{t+1}}{c_t}(1 + r_{t+1} - \delta)\right] \frac{c_t}{c_{t-1}} = 0, \tag{20}$$

since any zero factors multiplied by a factor of some observation will be zero.

Hence, the data are $\left\{\frac{c_{t+1}}{c_t}, r_{t+1}\right\}$, and the instruments $\left\{1, \frac{c_t}{c_{t-1}}\right\}.r_t$ could also have been used as an instrument. This implies that the average (first moments) of the data series is used in order to estimate parameter values.

When using GMM, the choice of instrument may impact the estimation. We may also have issues with unobserved variables. If analytical moment conditions are impossible or hard to obtain, they can be computed numerically by simulation (often called simulated GMM). This is particularly useful if there are unobservable variables in Euler equations such as the one above or there are nonlinear function of steady-state parameters. Further, a large sample is needed in order for asymptotic theory to apply, and Monte Carlo studies have not been favorable to GMM [26].

5. Full information maximum likelihood

In order to identify the structural parameters of the system (i.e. the complete theoretical model), the full system should be estimated. Full information maximum likelihood (FIML) estimation, such as, for example, in [26], can be used in order to estimate the parameters of new Keynesian models. Hence, this uses full information from the model rather than the limited information approach used in GMM, where we looked at some moment conditions. When using maximum likelihood, the estimated parameters will be the ones that provide the maximum of the likelihood function or the log of the likelihood function.

In general, the data (y) depend on the unknown parameters θ through a probability density function

$$y \sim f(y;\theta). \tag{21}$$

The estimator is then $\hat{\theta}$, and it is a function of the data

$$\hat{\theta} = g(y). \tag{22}$$

Given the observed y_0, the estimator is then obtained by the likelihood function

$$\hat{\theta} = \arg\max_{\theta} \{f(y_0;\theta)\}, \tag{23}$$

or the log of this function. We then get the value of θ that provides the maximum of $f(y_0;\theta)$. That is, the parametes that yield the maximum probability of observing y_0.

Since the equations in DSGE models typically are nonlinear, we need to solve the model first and obtain a linear representation of the model. This provides a system where all the endogenous variables are expressed as a function of the exogenous variables and parameters of the model. However, a linear approximation of the model is often solved instead. The variables are then represented as deviation from the theoretical steady state (see Section 2). The structural parameters are estimated, and the model is assumed to be the true data generating process, see, for example, [26] or [27].

Almost all log-linearized DSGE models have a state-space representation

$$\begin{aligned} x_t &= Ax_{t-1} + B\varepsilon_t \\ y_t &= Cx_t + D\eta_t, \end{aligned} \tag{24}$$

where x_t is a vector containing the endogenous and exogenous state variables, and y_t is a vector containing the observed variables. Hence, $y_t = \cdots$ is measurement equation, linking data to model. The objective is to estimate the parameter given the observed y_t. The error term $\eta_t \sim N(0,R)$ is independent of x_t, and $\varepsilon_t \sim N(0,Q)$ is independent of $x_0, x_1, \dots, x_t$ and $y_1, \dots, y_t$. Further, the matrices A, B, C, and D contain nonlinear functions of the structural parameters.

If both x_t and y_t contain observables, the state-space representation is a restricted VAR(1). If not, we may use a Kalman filter [28] in order to obtain the expected value of the unobservable variables and the likelihood function. This provides one-step-ahead forecast errors (in-sample) and the recursive variance of forecast errors. Hence, the Kalman filter gives the expected value of all of the potentially unobserved variables given the history of the unobserved variables.

FIML also has some limitations, depending on what the DSGE model looks like. Firstly, we need as many shocks as observable variables in order to perform the estimation. This is known as stochastic singularity, and we, thus, often need to add shocks or errors to the model in order to utilize the full potential of a data set with a lot of variables. The model in [20] has only one shock ε_t, but three observables $\{y_t, c_t, n_t\}$. We can, thus, add structural shocks or measurement errors to the model if we want to utilize data on all observables.

When using FIML, we assume that the model is the correct representation of the data generating process (DGP). Hence, FIML is sensitive to misspecification since we estimate the model under this assumption. We often also have partial or weak identification of parameters when using FIML, see, for example, [29]. Both of these issues may give an issue with "the dilemma of absurd parameter estimates" [30], which implies that FIML estimates of structural parameters can often be at odds with additional information economists may have.

6. Bayesian methods

Since DSGE models contain a lot of parameters and often use a relatively small sample of quarterly data, the likelihood function typically contains a lot of local maxima and minima and nearly flat surfaces [19], making identification hard. In order to circumvent this issue, DSGE models are often estimated using Bayesian estimation. This combines a prior distribution with a likelihood-based estimation such as FIML presented in the previous section. This, thus, takes some of the problems with maximum likelihood estimation into account. However, the estimated parameters using Bayesian methods do not necessarily reflect all of the information in the data since prior distributions will influence the estimates to some extent. Using priors may also hide identification problems, which is an issue often neglected when estimating DSGE models [29].

The main difference between FIML and Bayesian methods is the way data are treated or interpreted. In frequentist methods such as FIML, the parameters are fixed and the data are random. This allows us to estimate the variance of the estimator and their confidence intervals, that is. the interval that $\hat{\theta}$ lies in $1-\alpha$ percent of the time. Bayesian inference assumes that data are fixed and that the parameters are unknown. We may, therefore, focus on the variance of the parameter (rather than the variance of the estimator). Confidence intervals in Bayesian estimation will show the interval that has the highest probability of including θ conditional on the observed data, a prior distribution on θ, and a functional form (the DSGE model in our case).

If we have the model $f(x|\theta)$ and the prior $f(\theta)$, we want to find the posterior probability density function $f(\theta|x)$. Using Bayes' rule, we have

$$f(\theta|y) = \frac{f(y|\theta)f(\theta)}{f(y)} \tag{25}$$

$$f(\theta|y) \propto f(y|\theta)f(\theta). \tag{26}$$

Hence, the posterior kernel equals the model multiplied by the prior. We can, thus, find the distribution for the unknown parameter θ. Additionally, a point estimate of the posterior can be found, typically as the mean, median, or mode of the posterior distribution or by a loss function $\tilde{\theta} = \arg\min_{\hat{\theta}} E\{\mathcal{L}(\hat{\theta}-\theta)\}$. The mean squared error, the absolute error, and the max aposteriori will, respectively, yield the mean, median, and maximum of the posterior distribution. Bayesian estimation is, thus, a combination of maximum likelihood estimation and a prior distribution. It is also important to remember that the data are fixed when using Bayesian estimation. We do, therefore, not necessarily seek to use the results for generalizing purposes, while we try to find the parameter(s) that gives the highest probability of observing the data at hand when using maximum likelihood.

In Bayesian estimation, the aim is to find the posterior density function $f(\theta|y_0)$. This shows how the parameters θ depend on the data y. θ is assumed random, while it was assumed deterministic in the case of maximum likelihood estimation. A prior distribution function $f(\theta)_,$ thus, needs to be specified before estimation as this is combined with a likelihood estimation as in FIML. Prior distributions may be subjective or objective. Subjective priors are a result of subjective opinions, while objective priors can be priors found by microeconomic empirical studies [31]. The weight we put on the prior distribution relative to the likelihood function also needs to be chosen a priori. We, thus, have two extreme cases of Bayesian estimation: 1) No weight on the prior (e.g. flat priors), which will be similar to FIML, and 2) Full weight on the prior and none on the likelihood, consistent with calibration. Hence, Bayesian estimation can be considered a combination of calibration and FIML.

The posterior is simulated by an algorithm such as a Monte Carlo method, and the accepted parameter values will form a histogram, which can be smoothed to provide the posterior distribution function.

An advantage of Bayesian estimation is that we may avoid identification issues that often are a problem when using FIML. However, we are also prone to hide these issues, which may be a problem. As argued in [32], Bayesian estimates should be compared to FIML estimates in order to see what role the priors have. Another advantage of Bayesian estimation is that we do not need to assume that the model is the correct DGP as for FIML and GMM.

Using prior information may also be an advantage since this is available information that then is taken into account in the estimation process even if it is not part of the model or the data set used in the estimation. However, if the same data are used for prior information as for the Bayesian estimation, for example,. great ratios, the priors do not add any information. It is also possible to compare different models *via* posterior odds ratios, see [33].

However, it may be difficult to replicate results from Bayesian estimation due to computationally intensive simulation methods (Metropolis-Hastings algorithm) [18]. For an overview of recent developments in Bayesian methods, see [34].

7. The cointegrated VAR model

DSGE models often contain variables that are nonstationary such as prices, wages, GDP, and productivity, and we use a log-linearized model with stationary variables in order to estimate the model with FIML or Bayesian methods. The data are then usually filtered by, for example, . the Hodrick-Prescott or the band pass filter in order to separate the trend and the cyclical component of the nonstationary data series, see, for example, [17]. Hence, the cyclical component of a variable in the data should correspond to the deviation from steady state for a variable in the theoretical model and is then used in order to estimate the (log-linearized) DSGE model. While the filtered cycle measures deviations from an estimated trend, the log deviation in the theoretical model measures deviation from the theoretical steady state. Hence, there may be a mismatch between the trend component of the data and the theoretical trending relationships in the model, expressed by the steady-state relationships of the model. This should be taken into account when estimating DSGE models since the steady-state relationships are expected to correspond to the long-run relations of the observed variables.

We saw that the log-linear system may be solved to yield a purely backward-looking solution such that it is represented by a vector autoregressive (VAR) model containing cross-equations restrictions from the DSGE model if all of the variables are observables.[2] An estimated VAR model should, therefore, be similar to the solution of a new Keynesian model if the model is the true data generating process.

Since the solution of the DSGE model takes the form of a restricted VAR model, another approach for estimating such a model is to first estimate an unrestricted VAR model and then impose various restrictions on it from the theoretical DSGE model. This implies going from a general to a specific model, and it allows testing the restrictions as they are imposed on the unrestricted model. If the restrictions are rejected, the theoretical model can be modified such that it is more in line with the empirical observations.

A VAR model with k lags may be written as

$$Z_t = \Pi_1 Z_{t-1} + \cdots \Pi_k Z_{t-k} + \varepsilon_t, \tag{27}$$

where Z_t is a vector of observed variables. A DSGE model has this representation (typically with $k = 1$ lag) if all of its variables are observable as shown in (24). The VAR may be reformulated to a vector error correction model (VECM) such as

$$\Delta Z_t = \Gamma_1 \Delta Z_{t-1} + \cdots + \Gamma_{k-1} \Delta Z_{t-k+1} + \alpha \tilde{\beta}' \tilde{Z}_{t-1} + \gamma_0 + \gamma_1 t + \varepsilon_t, \tag{28}$$

where $\tilde{\beta}' = [\beta, \beta_0, \beta_1]$, $\tilde{Z}_{t-1} = [Z_{t-1}, 1, t]'$, $\varepsilon_t \sim IN(0, \Omega)$ for $t = 1, \dots, T$, and Z_{-1}, Z_0 is given. γ_0 is a constant. If there are one or more linear combinations of nonstationary (integrated of order one, $I(1)$) variables that are stationary (integrated of order zero, $I(0)$), they can be considered cointegration relationships. These are found by imposing reduced rank on the estimated VAR and will yield the cointegrated vector autoregressive (CVAR) model [36]. The cointegration rank is found through statistical tests and should match what is implied by theory (e.g. the number of steady-state relationships in the DSGE model). Common stochastic trends should cancel through steady-state relationships if they are driven by unit roots.

Additionally, the data do not need to be pre-filtered when using this approach since assumptions from the theoretical model on the stochastic trends may be tested and imposed. First, we find the number of cointegrating vectors in the data. These represent the long-run properties of the data and should correspond to the steady state of the theoretical model. The long-run properties of the model are then imposed as restrictions on the β vectors in the VECM eq. (28). There should, for example,. be a constant relationship between capital k and hours worked n and between consumption c and output y in the model in [20], as shown in eq. (11) and eq. (12).

---

[2] If only some variables are observed, it has a state space representation in form of a vector autoregressive regressive moving average (VARMA) model, see, for example, [35]).

For an example of this, see [37], which tests several restrictions from the theoretical DSGE model in [27] using the CVAR framework. Similar testing of the long-run properties of DSGE models can be found in [38, 39]. This is in line with using the VAR model as a statistical model and test theory through the probabilistic approach as suggested by [3], see, for example, [40].

Short-run restrictions may also be imposed and tested through cross-equation restrictions on the VAR representation of the data such as imposing the restrictions suggested by the parameters in (15). See [41] for an example of this. Using the CVAR model thereby allows using frequentist methods while dealing with potential misspecification. Hence, we do not need to use Bayesian methods if we would like to relax the assumption that the model is the true DGP as in GMM and FIML, but we can test it in the CVAR framework. If the restrictions from the DSGE model are rejected when tested in the CVAR model, this may suggest misspecification. The theoretical model can then be modified to be more in line with what we find empirically.

8. Conclusion

As shown in the chapter, calibration may be useful for assessing the relevance of a theoretical model by, for example, . simulations. This is often necessary if data are not available for many of the variables in the model. Calibration may also be used as a preliminary step in modeling and evaluation.

Generalized methods of moments do not require that we need to solve the model before estimation, and we do not need observations on all of the variables in the model. This avoids the problem of stochastic singularity, which is an issue when we use full information estimation methods. However, this also implies that we usually only focus on a subset of the model and relevant variables.

Full information maximum likelihood and Bayesian estimation both involve using the complete model (usually in a log-linearized form) and take full advantage of the data. While maximum likelihood may have identification issues for the structural parameters of the model, Bayesian methods can address this by using prior distributions for parameters. However, the choice of priors and the chosen prior weight may impact the estimates, and thus affect the estimates such that the data set at hand is not allowed to speak freely.

By using the cointegrated vector autoregressive model, we are able to test the theoretical implications of the model, in particular the long-run implications of a model, rather than assuming that the model is the true data generating process as with full information maximum likelihood or generalized method of moments. We also do not need to filter the data before estimating the model, removing the problem of a potential mismatch between the theoretical steady state and the long-run relationships in the data. Hence, if we would like to take full advantage of the data while also testing the implications from the model, the cointegrated vector autoregressive model is a relevant tool. We may use it as a preliminary step to assess the empirical relevance of a theoretical model or use it as a fully specified macroeconometric model.

Notes

This chapter has been written on the background of the trial lecture titled "Describe and compare different methods for analyzing DSGE models: Calibration,

GMM, FIML, Bayesian methods, and CVAR" for defending my Ph.D. in Economics at the Norwegian University of Science and Technology, as well as the introductory chapter from the thesis "Testing economic theory using the cointegrated vector autoregressive model: New Keynesian models and house prices", see [42].

Appendix

The methods illustrated in this chapter to evaluate and estimate Hansen's RBC model [20] is possible to carry out and investigate using available code.

For calibration of the model and estimation using full information maximum likelihood and Bayesian methods, the most convenient approach is perhaps to use Dynare code, available at Johannes Pfeifer's home page on Github: https://github.com/johannespfeifer/dsge_mod [43] For more information about Dynare, which is a program that you can run using Matlab or Octave, see www.dynare.org. For GMM estimation of Hansen's RBC model, see [44].

In order to test the long-run implications of a DSGE model, I have estimated a cointegrated VAR with quarterly data on output, consumption, hours worked, and capital from 1960 to 2002 using R. The code is shown below. The data set is available at [45] and was used in order to test the implications of the model in [27] by [37]. In the code below, there is a test of one of the long-run restrictions of Hansen's model found in the steady states for the output-to-consumption ratio using commands in the urca package [46] in R. I also include the dummy variables accounting for extraordinary institutional events used in [37] to specify the model.

```
alldata <– read.table(file = "irelanddata.csv",
                        sep = ";", header=TRUE).
logdata <– subset(alldata, select=c(qtr,Ly,Lc,Lh,LCapP)).
colnames(logdata)[colnames(ldata) == "LCapP"] ="Lk".
dummyvar <– read.table(file = "dummies.csv",
                        sep = ";", header=TRUE).
total <– merge(logdata,dummyvar,by="qtr").
attach(total).
data <– cbind(Ly,Lc,Lh,Lk).
dum <– cbind(Ds7801,Dp7003,Dp7403,Dp7404,Dp7801,Dtr8001).
cointd <– ca.jo(total, type='trace', K=2,
                  season=4, dumvar=dum).
summary(cointd).
H <- matrix(byrow=TRUE,
c(1,0,0,
–1,0,0,
0,1,0,
0,0,1), c(4,3)).
betarestrictions <– blrtest(z=cointd, H=H, r=1).
summary(betarestrictions).
```

First, the data are loaded into the object alldata. I then take the natural logarithm of the variables that are used and place them in logdata. The variable for capital is then renamed in order to match the theoretical model, which uses the letter k for capital. The dummy variables from a separate dummies.csv file matching the dummy variables from [37] are loaded into dummyvar, and the data are combined into the data

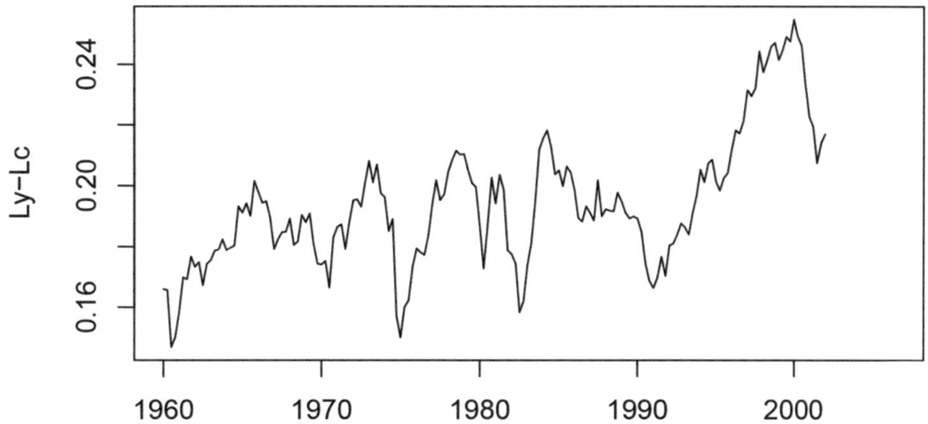

Figure 1.
Difference between log of income and log of consumption.

frame `total` and attached. The data are then separated into the endogenous variables in `data` and the exogenous dummy variables in `dum`.

By using the command `ca.jo`, I estimate the VAR model and test for the number of reduced rank. This is then set to $r = 2$ as in [37], and the restriction of a constant long-run relationship between Ly and Lc is imposed on the beta matrix.

The restriction of a stationary long-run relationship between consumption and income $(Ly - Lc \sim I(0))$ yields a p-value of 0, indicating that we reject it. This is perhaps not surprising, given the plot of the difference between log of income and log of consumption as shown in **Figure 1**, where we observe an upward trend and not stationarity.

Author details

Bjørnar Karlsen Kivedal
Østfold University College, Halden, Norway

*Address all correspondence to: bjornar.k.kivedal@hiof.no

References

[1] Tinbergen J. Business Cycles in the United States of America, 1919–1932. London: League of Nations, Economic Intelligence Service; 1939

[2] Frisch R. Propagation problems and impulse problems in dynamic economics. In: Economic Essays in Honour of Gustav Cassel. London: Allen and Unwin; 1933. pp. 171-205

[3] Haavelmo T. The probability approach in econometrics. Econometrica: Journal of the Econometric Society. 1944;**12**:1-114

[4] Haavelmo T. The statistical implications of a system of simultaneous equations. Econometrica, Journal of the Econometric Society. 1943;**11**(1):1-12

[5] Klein LR. Economic Fluctuations in the United States, 1921–1941. Vol. 176. New York: Wiley; 1950

[6] Klein LR, Goldberger AS. An Econometric Model of the United States, 1929–1952. Vol. 9. Amsterdam: North-Holland Publishing Company; 1955

[7] Welfe W. Macroeconometric Models. Advanced Studies in Theoretical and Applied Econometrics. Heidelberg: Springer Berlin; 2013

[8] Lucas RE. Econometric policy evaluation: A critique. Carnegie-Rochester Conference Series on Public Policy. 1976;**1**:19-46

[9] Kydland FE, Prescott EC. Time to build and aggregate fluctuations. Econometrica: Journal of the Econometric Society. 1982;**50**(6): 1345-1370

[10] Galí J. Monetary Policy, Inflation, and the Business Cycle: An Introduction to the New Keynesian Framework. Princeton and Oxford: Princeton Univ Pr; 2008

[11] Smets F, Wouters R. Shocks and frictions in us business cycles: A bayesian dsge approach. American Economic Review. 2007;**97**(3):586-606

[12] Smets F, Wouters R. An estimated dynamic stochastic general equilibrium model of the euro area. Journal of the European Economic Association. 2003; **1**(5):1123-1175

[13] Calvo GA. Staggered prices in a utility-maximizing framework. Journal of Monetary Economics. 1983;**12**(3): 383-398

[14] Blanchard O, Galí J. Real wage rigidities and the new Keynesian model. Journal of Money, Credit and Banking. 2007;**39**:35-65

[15] O. Blanchard and J. Galí, Labor markets and monetary policy: A new Keynesian model with unemployment, American Economic Journal: Macroeconomics, vol. 2, pp. 1–30, April 2010

[16] Canova F. Methods for Applied Macroeconomic Research. Princeton and Oxford: Princeton University Press; 2007

[17] DeJong DM, Dave C. Structural Macroeconometrics. Princeton and Oxford: Princeton University Press; 2007

[18] Tovar C. DSGE models and central banks, economics: The open-access. Open-Assessment E-Journal. 2009;**3**: 20090016. DOI: 10.5018/economics-ejournal.ja.2009-16

[19] Fernández-Villaverde J. The econometrics of DSGE models. SERIEs:

Journal of the Spanish Economic Association. 2010;**1**(1):3-49

[20] Hansen GD. Indivisible labor and the business cycle. Journal of Monetary Economics. 1985;**16**(3):309-327

[21] Galí J, Gertler M, López-Salido J. Robustness of the estimates of the hybrid New Keynesian Phillips curve. Journal of Monetary Economics. 2005;**52**(6): 1107-1118

[22] Galı J, Gertler M. Inflation dynamics: A structural econometric analysis. Journal of Monetary Economics. 1999; **44**(2):195-222

[23] Hansen LP. Large sample properties of generalized method of moments estimators. Econometrica: Journal of the Econometric Society. 1982;**50**(4): 1029-1054

[24] Christiano LJ, Eichenbaum M. Current real-business-cycle theories and aggregate labor-market fluctuations. The American Economic Review. 1992;**82**(3): 430-450

[25] Burnside C, Eichenbaum M, Rebelo S. Labor hoarding and the business cycle. Journal of Political Economy. 1993;**101** (2):245-273

[26] Lindé J. Estimating new-Keynesian Phillips curves: A full information maximum likelihood approach. Journal of Monetary Economics. 2005;**52**(6): 1135-1149

[27] P. N. Ireland, A method for taking models to the data, Journal of Economic Dynamics and Control, vol. 28, pp. 1205–1226, March 2004

[28] Kalman RE. A new approach to linear filtering and prediction problems. Journal of Basic Engineering. 1960;**82**: 13-45

[29] Canova F, Sala L. Back to square one: Identification issues in DSGE models. Journal of Monetary Economics. 2009; **56**(4):431-449

[30] An S, Schorfheide F. Bayesian analysis of dsge models. Econometric Reviews. 2007;**26**(2–4):113-172

[31] Del Negro M, Schorfheide F. Priors from general equilibrium models for VARS. International Economic Review. 2004;**45**(2):643-673

[32] Fukac M, Pagan A. Issues in adopting DSGE models for use in the policy process, Australian National University, Centre for Applied Macroeconomic Analysis. CAMA Working Paper. 2006; **10**:2006

[33] Rabanal P, Rubio-Ramírez JF. Comparing new keynesian models of the business cycle: A bayesian approach. Journal of Monetary Economics. 2005; **52**(6):1151-1166

[34] Fernández-Villaverde J, Guerrón-Quintana PA. Estimating dsge models: Recent advances and future challenges. Annual Review of Economics. 2021;**13**: 229-252

[35] Fernández-Villaverde J, Rubio-Ramirez JF, Sargent T, Watson MW. ABCs (and Ds) of understanding VARs. American Economic Review. 2007; **97**(3):1021-1026

[36] Johansen S. Statistical analysis of cointegration vectors. Journal of Economic Dynamics and Control. 1988; **12**(2):231-254

[37] Juselius K, Franchi M. Taking a DSGE model to the data meaningfully, economics: The open-access. Open-Assessment E-Journal. 2007;**1**:4

[38] Kivedal BK. A DSGE model with housing in the cointegrated VAR

framework. Empirical Economics. 2014; **47**(3):853-880

[39] Kivedal BK. A new keynesian framework and wage and price dynamics in the Usa. Empirical Economics. 2018; **55**(3):1271-1289

[40] Juselius K. The Cointegrated VAR Model. Methodology and Applications. New York: Oxford University Press; 2006

[41] Bårdsen G, Fanelli L. Frequentist evaluation of small dsge models. Journal of Business & Economic Statistics. 2015; **33**(3):307-322

[42] Kivedal BK. Testing Economic Theory Using the Cointegrated Vector Autoregressive Model: New Keynesian Models and House Prices. PhD thesis. Trondheim: Norwegian University of Science and Technology. Faculty of Social Sciences and Technology Management. Department of Economics; 2013

[43] Johannes Pfeifer's home page on Github. https://github.com/johannespfeifer/dsge_mod [Accessed: March 24, 2023]

[44] Burnside AC. Real Business Cycle Models: Linear Approximation and GMM Estimation. Washington, D.C.: Mimeo, The World Bank; 1999

[45] Juselius K and Franchi M. Taking a DSGE Model to the Data Meaningfully [Dataset]. 2009

[46] Pfaff B, Zivot E, Stigler M, Pfaff MB. Package urca, unit root and cointegration tests for time series data. R Package Version. 2016:1-2. Available from: http://cran.pau.edu.tr/web/packages/urca/urca.pdf

Chapter 2

A Primer on Machine Learning Methods for Credit Rating Modeling

Yixiao Jiang

Abstract

Using machine learning methods, this chapter studies features that are important to predict corporate bond ratings. There is a growing literature of predicting credit ratings via machine learning methods. However, there have been less empirical studies using ensemble methods, which refer to the technique of combining the prediction of multiple classifiers. This chapter compares six machine learning models: ordered logit model (OL), neural network (NN), support vector machine (SVM), bagged decision trees (BDT), random forest (RF), and gradient boosted machines (GBMs). By providing an intuitive description for each employed method, this chapter may also serve as a primer for empirical researchers who want to learn machine learning methods. Moody's ratings were employed, with data collected from 2001 to 2017. Three broad categories of features, including financial ratios, equity risk, and bond issuer's cross-ownership relation with the credit rating agencies, were explored in the modeling phase, performed with the data prior to 2016. These models were tested on an evaluation phase, using the most recent data after 2016.

Keywords: machine learning, credit ratings, forecasting, random forest, gradient boosted machine

1. Introduction

An issue of continuing interest to many financial market participants (portfolio risk managers, for example) is to predict corporate bond ratings for unrated issuers. Issuers themselves may seek a preliminary estimate of what their rating might be to decide the ratio of debt and equity financing. Starting with the seminal works of [1, 2], pioneering studies in the finance literature use accounting ratios and other publicly available information in reduced-form models to predict credit ratings. A variety of statistical techniques (OLS, discriminant analysis, and ordered logit/probit models) were employed to identify the most important characteristics for predicting ratings. See, [3–5].

Bond rating is, in a way, a classification problem. There is also a growing literature of predicting credit ratings via machine learning (ML) methods [6–11]. As can be seen from **Table 1**, neural network (NN) and support vector machine (SVM) have been

Study	Rating Categories	Methods	Data	Accuracy	Predictors	Sample size	Benchmark Models
[7]	5	SVM, NN	Bank Ratings	~80%	21 Financial Ratios	265 (US) +74 (Taiwan)	LR:~ 75%
[8]	6	NN	Moody's long term ratings on US firms	79%	25 financial ratios	129	LDA: 33%
[9]	5	SVM	Ratings on commercial papers in Korea	67.2%	297 financial ratios	3017	NN: 59.9%, MDA: 58.8%, CBR: 63.4%
[6]	9	SVM	International bank ratings	62.4%	7 financial ratios, time and county dummies		Ordered Logit: 51.5%, Ordered Probit: 50.8%
[11]	3	RF + RST	enterprise credit ratings in Taiwan	93.4%	21 financial variable + distance to default	2470	RST: 90.3%, RF + DT: 84%, DT: 83.5% RF + SVM: 77.8%, SVM: 74.4%
[10]	7	LASSO	CDS-based and equity-based ratings	84% and 91%	268 financial factors, market-driven indicators, and macroeconomic predictors	1298 + 1540	Ordered Probit: 22% + 49%

Note: SVM = Support Vector Machine. NN = Neural Network. MDA = Multivariate Discriminant Analysis. RF = Random Forest. RST = Rough Set Theory.

Table 1.
Summary of credit rating predictive studies using machine learning.

widely employed by prior studies. However, there have been less empirical studies using *ensemble methods*, which refer to the technique of combining the prediction of multiple classifiers. This study attempts to fill the void by employing three ensemble methods to predict credit ratings and contrasting their performance with popular single-classifier ML methods.

The two popular methods for creating accurate ensembles are bootstrap aggregating, or bagging, and boosting. Previous works in the statistics and computer science literature have shown that these methods are very effective for decision trees (DT)[1], so this chapter considers DT as the basic classification method. [11] employs the random forest (RF) to predict enterprise ratings in Taiwan. To date, no comparative study has been carried out for the United States with any ensemble methods to our knowledge. Other than RF, this study also employs two additional ensemble methods: bagged decision trees (BDT) and gradient boosted machine (GBM).

This study is also the first to explore the predictive power of conflicts of interest in forecasting bond ratings. After the collapse of highly rated securities during the 07–09

[1] See, for example, [12–14].

financial crisis, the role of credit rating agencies (CRAs) as gatekeepers to financial markets has been scrutinized by academia and regulators at an unprecedented level. A number of conflicts of interest, including the issuer-pays business model, cross-ownership [15, 16], non-rating business relationship [17], transitioning analysts [18], have been identified in the literature as contributing factors to the rating inflation.

The type of conflict of interest under study arises from cross-ownership, meaning that the bond issuers and the CRA are controlled by common shareholders. Conflicts of interest between shareholders and managers, at a general level, have a variety of negative impact on the company [19]. In the context of the rating industry, as noted by [16], companies invested by Moody's two large shareholders, Berkshire Hathaway and Davis Selected Advisors, tend to receive more favorable ratings compared with others. Based on institutional ownership data, [15] constructed an index to capture bond issuers' cross-ownership with Moody's via all common shareholders and finds such biases to be more universal.

Motivated by the aforementioned studies, this chapter incorporates several conflicts of interest measure from the cross-ownership channel to predict Moody's ratings from 2001 to 2017. Since the predictive performance of ML methods is usually context-dependent, we compare the aforementioned tree-based ensemble methods (RF, BDT, and GBM) with three other ML models: ordered logit model (OL), neural network (NN), and support vector machine (SVM). RF presents the best results, correctly predicting 73.2% ratings out of sample. To improve the interpretability of "black box" ML models, we use sensitivity analysis to measure the importance and effect of particular input features in the model output response.

The rest of the chapter is organized as follow. Section 2 describes the empirical rating data and the features (attributes) under study. Section 3 discusses the three ensemble ML methods in the context of predicting credit ratings. Section 4 contains the predictive results and sensitivity analyses, and Section 5 concludes.

2. Data and features

The objective of this chapter is to predict corporate bond ratings assigned by Moody's, the leading credit rating agency (CRA) in the United States. The empirical sample consists of publicly listed companies covered in either Center for Research in Security Prices (CRSP) or Compustat. Moody's ratings on bonds issued by these companies are obtained from Mergent's Fixed Income Securities Database (FISD). Since the analysis involves Moody's shareholders, the sampling period starts from January 2001, when Moody's went to public, to December 2017.

2.1 Credit rating outcome

Under Moody's rating scale, the rating outcome falls into seven ordered categories with descending credit quality: Aaa,Aa,A,Baa,Ba,B, and C. The first four categories, from Aaa to Baa, are termed "investment-grade," whereas the remaining three are termed "high yield." The distribution of ratings over time is reported in **Table 2**. In 2004, about 50% of bonds in the data received investment grade ratings. The proportion of investment grade bonds has been trending up prior to the 07–09 financial crisis. The fact that nearly 90% of bonds received investment grade rating in 2008 suggests an obvious inflation of ratings. For the purpose of predicting credit ratings, it

Year	*Aaa*	*Aa*	*A*	*Baa*	*Ba*	*B*	C	*Total # of Ratings*
2001	6	17	62	125	59	44	2	315
2002	1	8	57	93	52	39	2	252
2003	8	47	67	117	54	98	12	403
2004	3	11	44	94	53	73	8	286
2005	1	21	39	93	51	49	9	263
2006	3	19	69	106	41	41	20	299
2007	6	24	103	95	41	45	4	318
2008	2	29	76	96	21	5	1	230
2009	3	15	97	164	57	73	7	416
2010	7	24	71	134	59	82	20	397
2011	10	17	117	163	33	69	12	421
2012	3	24	134	189	69	89	14	522
2013	12	29	150	218	76	76	15	576
2014	8	20	127	231	59	65	10	520
2015	20	22	178	274	53	46	3	596
2016	26	31	160	278	62	57	1	615
2017	11	31	98	166	41	36	2	385
Total	130	389	1649	2636	881	987	142	6814

Table 2.
Distribution of ratings.

is therefore important to include conflicts of interest measures, which account for this trend.

A second observation from **Table 2** is that the rating outcome is highly skewed toward the middle. The majority of bonds are rated in *A* and *Baa*, and only 2% of bonds received *Aaa* or *C* ratings. This is yet another reason to consider ensemble methods, which are known to be superior than other ML methods with single classifiers when applying to highly imbalanced data [20, 21].

2.2 Attributes under study

For each quarter from 2001Q1 to 2017Q4, a total of 20 features/attributes are obtained from a variety of sources to predict ratings. These features can be broadly categorized into three groups: (1) financial ratios, (2) equity risk measures, and (3) the bond issuer's "connectedness" with Moody's shareholders.

2.2.1 Financial ratios

We follow [22] and employ the following financial ratios in the analysis: (X1) the value of the firm's total assets (*log(asset)*), (X2) long- and short-term debt divided by total asset (*Book_lev*). (X3) Convertible debt divided by total assets (*ConvDe_assets*), (X4) rental payments divided by total assets (*Rent_Assets*), (X5) cash and marketable securities divided by total assets (*Cash_assets*), (X6) long- and short-term debt divided by EBITDA (*Debt_EBITDA*), (X7) EBITDA to interest payments (*EBITA_int*), (X8) profitability, measured as EBITDA divided by sales (*Profit*), (X9) tangibility, measured as net property, plant, and equipment divided by total assets (*PPE_assets*), (X10) capital expenditures divided by total assets (*CAPX_assets*), (X11) the volatility of profitability (*Vol_profit*), defined as the standard deviation of profitability in the last 5 years divided by the mean in absolute values. The data on the aforementioned firm-level financial ratios are obtained from the CRSP-Compustat merged database in Wharton Research and Data Services (WRDS).

There is a distinction between the issuer rating and issue rating for corporate bonds. The former addresses the issuer's overall credit creditworthiness, whereas the latter refers to specific debt obligations and considers the ranking in the capital structure such as secured or subordinated.[2] Since this chapter predicts rating at the bond level, three bond characteristics are also included: (X12) the log of the issuing amount (*Amt*), (X13) a dummy variable indicating whether the bond is senior (*Seniority*), and (X14) a dummy variable indicating whether the bond is secured (*Security*). The issuing amount affects the maximum financial loss on the investment, whereas the seniority and security status affect the priority of repayment should a default occur. Data on these bond characteristics are obtained from FSID along with the credit ratings.

2.2.2 Equity risk

As noted by [23], equity risk has been accounting for a greater proportion of variations in credit rating outcomes among the three leading CRAs in the United States. To obtain measures for a company's equity risk, we estimate a Fama–French three-factor model for each issuer in the sample.[3] The following measures are then obtained: (X15) the firm's beta (*Beta*), which is the stock's market beta computed estimated annually using the CRSP value-weighted index, and (X16) the firm's idiosyncratic risk (*Idiosyncratic risk*), computed annually as the root mean squared error from the three-factor model.

2.2.3 Cross-ownership with Moody's

As noted above, conflicts of interest are measured by the "connectedness" (cross-ownership) between Moody's and a bond issuer. To characterize the degree of cross-ownership, I first obtain the list of Moody's shareholders from Thomson Reuters (13F) and calculate their ownership stake in Moody's (the percentage of Moody's stock that they hold) for each quarter in the sampling period. Next, I access each shareholder's investment portfolio to find out which bond issuers have the same shareholders as investors. The shareholder's manager type code (MGRNO) and the firm's Committee on Uniform Securities Identification Procedures (CUSIP) number are used to match the shareholding data with bond issuers.

To summarily characterize the shared-ownership relation between bond issuers and Moody's, I employ the following measure, termed *Moody-Firm-Ownership-Index*

---

[2] The issuer rating usually applies to senior unsecured debt

[3] The normal estimation window is set to be 252 days prior to the rating assignment date. For companies with sparse stock price data, we require at least 126 days.

(MFOI), proposed by [15]. Suppose Moody's has $j = 1,2,\cdots,M$ shareholders in a given quarter[4], and any subset of those shareholders can invest in an issuing firm. Define

$$(X17): \quad MFOI_i = \sum_{j=1}^{M} b_{ij} s_j \tag{1}$$

where s_j denotes shareholder j's ownership take in Moody's, and b_{ij} denotes bond issuer i's weight in shareholder j's investment portfolio. Note that $b_{ij} = 0$ means shareholder j does not invest in bond issuer i.

In addition to MFOI, three other measures are included as predictors. The first is the number of common shareholders, defined as

$$(X18): \quad Num\_SH_i = \sum_{j=1}^{M} \mathbf{1}\{b_{ij} > 0\} \tag{2}$$

The second is the number of large common shareholders (which owns at least 5% of Moody's stock), defined as

$$(X19): \quad Num\_large\_SH_i = \sum_{j=1}^{M} \mathbf{1}\{b_{ij} > 0\} \times \mathbf{1}\{s_j > 0.05\} \tag{3}$$

The last is a dummy variable capturing if the bond issuer is invested by Berkshire Hathaway, Moody's leading shareholder for our sampling period.

$$(X20): \quad BRK_i = \mathbf{1}\{b_{ik} > 0\}, \quad k = \text{Berkshire Hathaway} \tag{4}$$

Berkshire Hathaway is singled out here because it owns significantly more shares of Moody's compared with any other large shareholders.

2.3 Descriptive statistics

After combining data from multiple sources, the final dataset consists of 6817 bonds issued by 895 firms. The descriptive statistics for the 20 features/attributes are reported in **Table 3**. For asset (X_1), EBITDA to interest (X_7), profitability (X_8), issuing amount (X_{12}), and seniority (X_{13}), there is a clear positive correlation between rating categories and the level of these attributes. For others like the Book-leverage ratio (X_2), Debt-to-EBITDA ratio (X_6), tangibility-to-asset ratio (X_{10}), volatility of profit (X_{11}), and idiosyncratic risk (X_{16}), the correlation is negative. For the four conflicts of interest measures (X_{17} - X_{20}), they all decrease as the rating drops.

3. Methods

The dataset is split into two subsets based on the timing of the rating: a training set, which consists of 5814 (85.3% of the total) ratings before 2016, and a holdout set, which consists of 1000 (14.7%) ratings in 2016–2017. In this section, we discuss the

[4] Since all of the variable are time-specific, I drop the time t subscript for notational simplicity

	Aaa	*Aa*	*A*	*Baa*	*Ba*	*B*	*C*
Financial Ratio							
Asset(X_1)	11.91	12.13	10.69	9.85	8.68	7.99	7.75
Book_lev (X_2)	0.18	0.33	0.29	0.32	0.36	0.46	0.59
ConvDe_asset (X_3)	0.00	0.00	0.00	0.01	0.02	0.02	0.04
Rent_asset(X_4)	0.01	0.01	0.01	0.01	0.01	0.02	0.02
Cash_asset(X_5)	0.28	0.12	0.13	0.08	0.09	0.09	0.09
Debt_ebitda(X_6)	1.42	5.45	3.14	3.03	2.90	3.85	6.66
Ebitda_int (X_7)	48.64	27.62	20.26	10.82	6.79	4.21	2.50
Profit(X_8)	0.31	0.31	0.27	0.23	0.19	0.19	0.24
PPE_asset(X_9)	0.22	0.21	0.25	0.32	0.31	0.36	0.46
CAPEX_asset (X_{10})	0.04	0.04	0.04	0.05	0.05	0.06	0.08
Profit_vol (X_{11})	0.06	0.06	0.11	0.13	0.19	0.18	0.01
Amt(X_{12})	13.92	13.11	13.27	13.12	12.84	12.68	12.37
Seniority(X_{13})	0.99	0.99	0.99	0.98	0.88	0.81	0.82
Secure(X_{14})	0.01	0.00	0.00	0.01	0.05	0.10	0.06
Equity Risk							
Beta(X_{15})	0.82	1.10	1.00	0.87	1.11	1.33	1.54
Idiosyncratic risk(X_{16})	0.06	0.07	0.08	0.08	0.12	0.14	0.17
Conflicts of Interest							
MFOI × 10,000 (X_{17})	87.48	59.30	24.32	8.54	2.31	1.11	0.74
Num_SH(X_{18})	335.41	281.01	269.72	217.16	144.40	101.76	94.87
Num_large_SH(X_{19})	1.59	1.40	1.18	0.95	0.80	0.74	0.76
BRK(X_{20})	0.32	0.30	0.06	0.03	0.02	0.01	0.01

Table 3.
Descriptive statistics by rating categories.

methodological aspect of three resemble methods—Random Forest (RF), Bagging, and Gradient Boosted Modeling (GBM)—and how they are implemented. The performances of these methods are compared with three other ML models: Ordered Logit Regression (OLR), Support Vector Machine (SVM), and Neural Network (NN), based on the predictive accuracy in the holdout set.

3.1 Decision trees

To understand the resemble method, we must first understand decision trees, the basic classification procedure upon which the ensemble (or resulting classification) is based[5]. For illustrative purpose, consider a sample decision tree that includes categorical outcome Y (credit rating) and three predictor variables: firm asset, leverage, and

[5] In this study, we restrict our attention to tree-based resemble methods because decision trees are extremely fast to train.

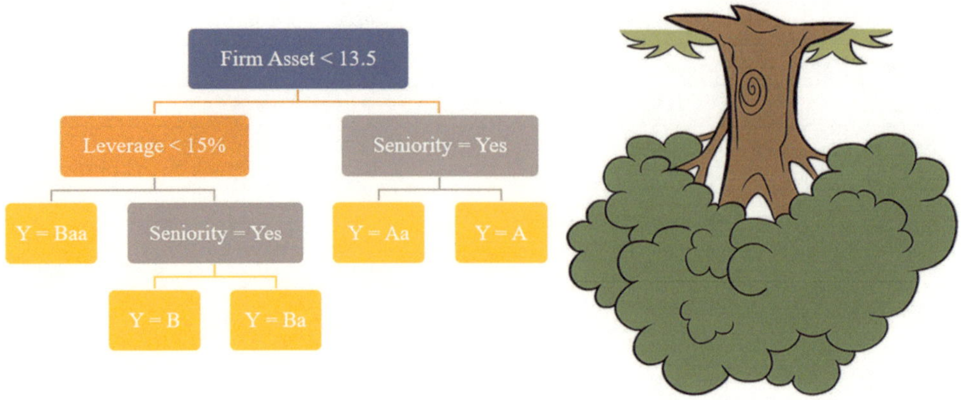

Figure 1.
Sample decision tree.

seniority (binary). As displayed in **Figure 1**, the main components of a decision tree model are nodes and branches, while the complexity of the decision tree is governed by splitting, stopping, and pruning.

Nodes There are three types of nodes. (a) A root node, also called a decision node, represents the most important feature (in this case, the level of log (firm asset)) that will lead all subdivisions. (b) Leaf nodes, also called end nodes, represent the final predicted rating outcome based on the sequence of divisions. (c) Internal nodes, also called chance nodes, represent the intermediate sequence of features that guide the classification.

Branches A decision tree model is formed using a hierarchy of branches, with the more important features displayed closer to the root node. Each path from the root node through internal nodes to a leaf node represents a classification decision sequence. These decision tree pathways can also be represented as "if-then" rules, with the left branch denoting the binary condition is met. For example, "if the natural log of firm asset is less than 13.5 and the leverage ratio is less than 15%, then the bond is rated as Baa."

Splitting Measures that are related to the degree of "purity" of the subsequent nodes (i.e., the proportion with the target condition) are used to choose between different potential input variables; these measures include entropy, Gini index, classification error, information gain, and gain ratio. Normally not all potential input variables will be used to build the decision tree model and in some cases a specific input variable may be used multiple times at different levels of the decision tree.

Stopping and Prunning An overly complex tree can result in each leaf node 100% pure (i.e., all bonds have the same rating), but is likely to suffer from the problem of overfitting. To prevent this from happening, one may grow a large tree first and then prune it to optimal size by removing nodes that provide less additional information. One parameter that controls the complexity is the number of leaf nodes.

3.2 Bagging

The decision trees discussed above suffer from high variance, meaning if the training data are split into multiple parts at random with the same decision tree applied to each, the predictive results can be quite different. Bootstrap aggregation, or bagging, is a technique used to reduce the variance of predictions by combining the result of multiple classifiers modeled on different subsamples of the same dataset. When applying bagging to decision trees, usually the trees are grown deep and are not pruned. Hence, each individual tree has high variance, but low bias. Averaging hundreds or even thousands of trees can reduce the variance and improve the predictive performance.

In practice, different subsamples are drawn from the training set with replacement (See, [24] for a detailed discussion of the bagging sampling approach). Each subsample has the same size with the training set, but only contains 2/3 of the data of the original data on average. The number of bootstrapped sample is therefore a hyperparameter to be tuned. For each bootstrapped sample, we fit a "bushy" deep decision tree with all 20 features considered at each splitting. Each tree acts as a base classifier to determine the rating of a bond. The final prediction is done via "majority voting" where each classifier casts one vote for its predicted rating, then the category with the most votes is used to classify the credit rating.

3.3 Random forest

Random forest is another ensemble classification method developed by [25]. One advantage of random forest (RF) over bagging is that it reduces the correlation among trees by randomizing the number of features. RF combines the bagging sampling approach of [24] and the random selection of features, introduced independently by [26, 27], to construct a collection of decision trees with controlled variation. Specifically, [25] recommends to randomly select $m = log_2(p + 1)$ features at any given splitting, with p being the total number of features, to grow each individual tree. Moreover, each tree is constructed using a subsample of the training set with replacement.

For the purpose of illustration, in **Figure 2**, we consider an RF populated by three trees that are similar to the one described in **Figure 1**. Note that the total number of features is 3. In this case, $m = log_2(4) = 2$, so each tree is generated using two features. For a bond with firm asset = 12, seniority = yes, and leverage = 12%, the majority rule returns a predicted rating of *Ba* category. In practice, the complexity of the random forest is governed by several hyperparameters, such as the number of trees and the maximum features at each splitting.

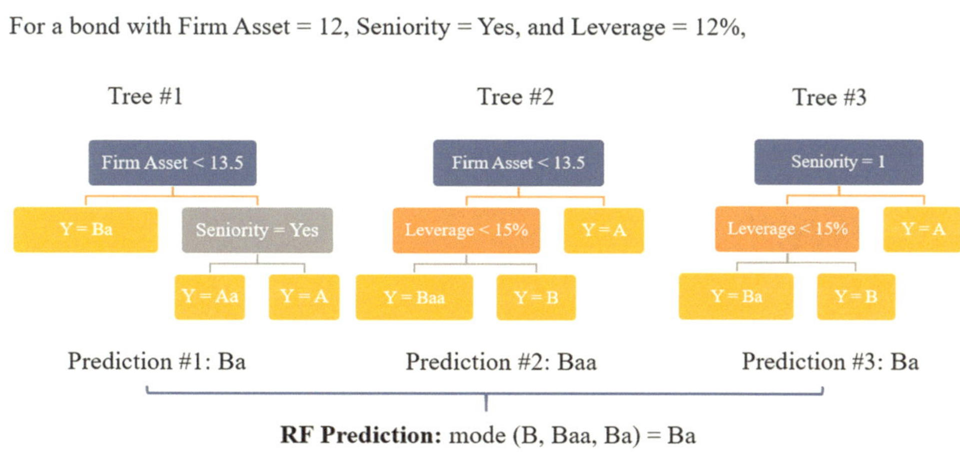

Figure 2.
Sample random forest.

3.4 Gradient boosting machines

Gradient Boosting Machines (GBMs) are a ensemble method, which recognizes the weak learners and attempts to strengthen those learners in a recursive manner to improve prediction. The key difference between GBM and Bagging is that the training stage is parallel for Bagging (i.e., each tree is built independently), whereas GBM builds the new tree in a sequential way. Specifically, when the first tree is generated, the residual errors are calculated and used in the next tree as the target variable. The predictions made by this last last tree are combined with the previous model's predictions. New residuals are calculated using the predicted value and the actual value. This process is repeated until the errors no longer decreased significantly.

During the prediction stage, bagging and RF simply average the individual predictions (the "majority rule"). In contrast, a new set of weights will be assigned to each tree in GBM. The final predicted rating is an weighted average of individual predictions. A tree with a good classification result on the training data will be assigned a higher weight than a poor one. There is no consensus regarding to which method is better than the other; the answer very much depends on the data and the researcher's objective. Some scholars have argued that gradient boosted trees can outperform random forest [28, 29]. Others believe boosting tends to aggregate the overfitting problem because repeatedly fitting the residuals can capture noisy information.

4. Results

In this section, we begin by comparing the three aforementioned ensemble methods (BDT, RF, and GBM) in terms of the out-of-sample predictive accuracy. Three non-ensemble ML methods, the ordered-logit model, support vector machine, and neural network, are also evaluated with the same dataset. For each employed method, we discuss the relevant hyperparameters and how they are tuned empirically.

All ML methods were implemented using the software R. To be specific, BDT and RF were implemented using the *randomForest* package. The number of features is fixed at all 20 for BDT. For RF, each tree randomly selects $m = log_2(20 + 1) = 5$ features. GBM is implemented using the package *gbm* package. For the three non-ensemble ML methods, ordered-logit model is implemented using the *polr* function from the *MASS* package. Support Vector Machine is implemented via the *svm* function from the *e1071* package. The neural network is implemented using the *neuralnet* package.

4.1 Predictive results

Bagged Decision Tree (BDT) To evaluate the predictive results, we report the classification matrix in the holdout sample for each employed method. In the case of BDT, the main hyperparameter needs to be tuned is the number of trees. We run three BDTs, setting the number of trees to be 200, 500, and 800. It is found the model with 500 trees has the highest predictive accuracy (=69.1%). The full classification matrix is reported in **Table 4**. The horizontal dimension represents the true rating received in the holdout sample, whereas the vertical dimension represents the predicted rating category. Therefore, the entries on the diagonal line capture the number of ratings

	Actual Ratings						
Predicted	**Aaa**	**Aa**	**A**	**Baa**	**Ba**	**B**	**C**
Aaa	19	0	0	0	0	0	0
Aa	0	28	8	0	0	0	0
A	4	3	148	15	2	1	0
Baa	14	31	95	390	39	9	0
Ba	0	0	7	22	35	13	0
B	0	0	0	17	27	70	2
C	0	0	0	0	0	0	1
Total	37	62	258	444	103	93	3
Accuracy							69.1%

Table 4.
The classification confusion matrix of BDT with 500 trees in holdout sample.

correctly predicted for a particular category. For example, the numbers in the first column shall be interpreted as 19 Aaa bonds are correctly classified as Aaa, whereas four (14) are misclassified into A (Baa).

Random Forest (RF) The next predictive model under evaluation is the Random Forest. In addition to the bagging technique, RF also randomizes the features set to further decrease the correlation among the decision trees. As noted above, RF has five hyperparameters that govern the complexity of the model. To decide these hyperparameter values, we implement a five-dimensional grid search where every combination of hyperparameters of interest is assessed. The hyperparameter grid is generated by

$$\mathcal{G} = \{m \times N \times n \times p \times r\}, \qquad \text{where} \tag{5}$$

- $m \in (3,4,5,6,7,8)$ is the number of features to consider at any given split.
- $N \in (1,2,3)$ is the minimum number of Nodes in each tree
- $n \in (200,500,800)$ is the number of trees in the forest.
- $p \in (0.6,0.8,1)\times$ (size of the training set) amount of data to generate each tree.
- $r = 1/0$ (with or without replacement in the sampling).

Consequently, a total of 216 (= $6 \times 2 \times 3 \times 2 \times 3$) specifications of RF are compared in terms of the predictive accuracy in the holdout set. As shown in **Table 5**, the best predictive model consists of 500 trees, with each tree generated from the entire training set ($p = 1$) with replacement. In each splitting, $m = 4$ features are randomly selected. The overall classification accuracy of the holdout data turned out to be 73.2%. From the classification confusion matrix in **Table 6**, RF has a reliable predictive performance in almost all rating categories.

To develop some sense of how RF make prediction, **Figure 3** plots one decision tree from the RF model. There are a total of six attributes used in this particular tree. MFOI

	Hyperparameters					Evaluation	
Model ID	m	N	n	r	p	RMSE	% of correct prediction
158	4	1	500	TRUE	1	0.259	0.732
5	7	1	200	TRUE	0.6	0.283	0.729
80	4	3	200	TRUE	0.8	0.277	0.728
152	4	3	200	TRUE	1	0.271	0.728
146	4	1	200	TRUE	1	0.262	0.723
176	4	3	800	TRUE	1	0.266	0.723
3	5	1	200	TRUE	0.6	0.285	0.722
170	4	1	800	TRUE	1	0.261	0.722
112	6	1	200	FALSE	0.8	0.263	0.720
86	4	1	500	TRUE	0.8	0.270	0.719

Table 5.
The 10 best RF models from hyperparameters tunning.

	Actual Ratings						
Predicted	Aaa	Aa	A	Baa	Ba	B	C
Aaa	19	1	0	0	0	0	0
Aa	0	38	9	0	0	0	0
A	18	23	171	15	2	0	0
Baa	0	0	78	413	49	16	0
Ba	0	0	0	7	33	20	0
B	0	0	0	9	19	57	2
C	0	0	0	0	0	0	1
Total	37	62	258	444	103	93	3
Accuracy							73.2%

Table 6.
The classification confusion matrix of the best RF in holdout sample.

and idiosyncratic risk appear to be the two most important attributes. From the rightmost terminal node, it is almost certain that bonds with MFOI < 1.7 and idiosyncratic risk > 0.1 can only receive high-yield ratings (25% Ba +57% B + 10% C = 91% of high yield), irrespective of other features. This provides a remarkably parsimonious yet robust decision rule to decide whether a bond is investment grade or not.

Gradient Boosting Machine (GBM) The classification confusion matrix of GBM is reported in **Table 7**. The overall predictive accuracy is 64.4%, which is 5 percentage point lower than BDT and nearly 10 percentage point lower than RF. As noted by [30], predictive results from Boosting methods are usually more volatile. [14] also made a conjecture that Boosting's sensitivity to noise may be partially responsible for its occasional increase in errors. As such, we recommend to always use RF or BDT for predicting credit ratings.

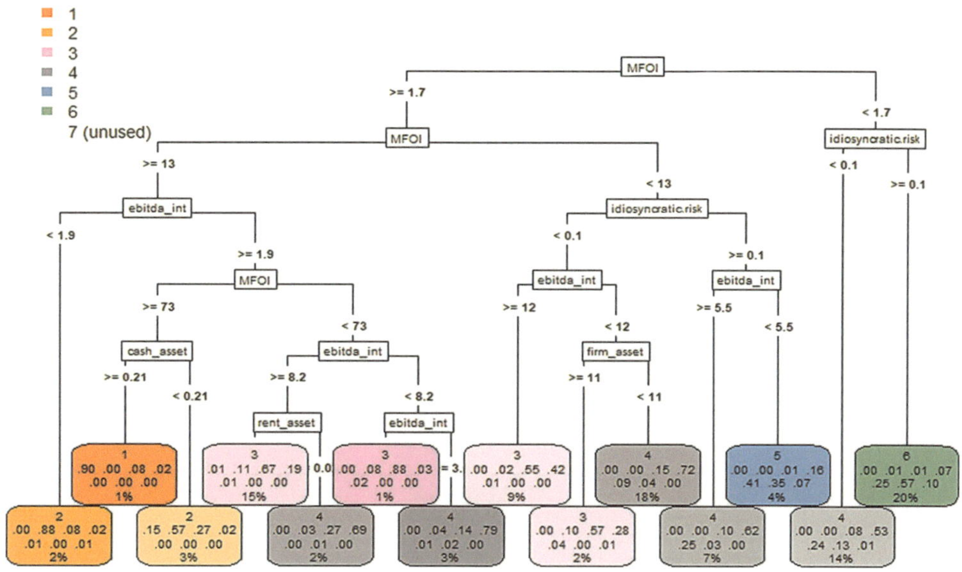

Figure 3.
Decision tree extracted from the RF model.

	Actual Ratings						
Predicted	**Aaa**	**Aa**	**A**	**Baa**	**Ba**	**B**	**C**
Aaa	0	0	0	0	0	0	0
Aa	0	7	5	0	0	0	0
A	35	28	174	33	6	0	0
Baa	2	27	74	370	40	10	0
Ba	0	0	1	23	32	19	0
B	0	0	4	18	25	61	3
C	0	0	0	0	0	3	0
Total	37	62	258	444	103	93	3
Accuracy							64.4%

Table 7.
The classification confusion matrix of GBM in holdout sample.

Ordered Logistic Regression (OLR) The OLR is a regression model where different features affect the rating outcome through the logistic transformation. Let $Z_i = \beta_0 + \sum_{j=1}^{20} x_{ij}\beta_j$ be a linear index summarizing the information of the 20 considered features where the β coefficients are to be estimated from the data. The predicted probability in OLR for each rating category, $k = 1, \cdots, 7$, can be described as $Pr(Y_{ik} = 1|x_i) = \frac{1}{1+exp\,(Z_i-\kappa_k)} - \frac{1}{1+exp\,(Z_i-\kappa_{k-1})}$ where κ_k is a series of threshold point separating the different ratings with $k_0 = -\infty$ and $k_7 = \infty$. While the model is easier to interpret, it is quite rigid and cannot accomodate complex nonlinear relationships.

The classification matrix of OLR is reported in **Table 8**. The overall classification accuracy is 53.9% for the holdout sample, which is much worse than RF. The model also fails to correctly predict all 37 *Aaa* bonds. This is unsurprising: when fitting a linear trend in the data (OLR belongs to the family of generalized linear model because the logistic transformation is applied on a linear score function of features), the fitness is usually worse in the tails of the distribution (**Table 9**).

Support Vector Machine (SVM) developed by [31] seeks to find the optimal separating hyperplane between binary classes by following the maximized margin criterion. When it comes to multiclass prediction where the outcome variables take k distinct categories, one may induce $\frac{k(k-1)}{2}$ individual binary classifiers and then use the majority rule to determine the final predicted outcome. In order to find the separating hyperplane, SVM uses a kernel function to enlarge the feature space using basis

	Actual Ratings						
Predicted	**Aaa**	**Aa**	**A**	**Baa**	**Ba**	**B**	**C**
Aaa	0	3	0	0	0	0	0
Aa	23	21	3	0	0	0	0
A	14	18	140	110	2	0	0
Baa	0	20	115	322	69	27	0
Ba	0	0	0	7	17	25	0
B	0	0	0	5	15	38	2
C	0	0	0	0	0	3	1
Total	37	62	258	444	103	93	3
Accuracy							53.9%

Table 8.
The classification confusion matrix of OLR in holdout sample.

	Actual Ratings						
Predicted	**Aaa**	**Aa**	**A**	**Baa**	**Ba**	**B**	**C**
Aaa	26	1	0	0	0	0	0
Aa	0	8	8	3	0	0	0
A	11	34	189	58	11	0	0
Baa	0	7	59	348	39	7	0
Ba	0	0	0	6	31	12	0
B	0	12	2	29	22	70	3
C	0	0	0	0	0	4	0
Total	37	62	258	444	103	93	3
Accuracy							67.2%

Table 9.
The classification confusion matrix of SVM in holdout sample.

functions. Mathematically, SVM can be viewed as the following constrained maximization problem,

$$min_{\alpha} \quad \frac{1}{2}\alpha^T Q\alpha - e^T\alpha \tag{6}$$

$$\text{s.t} \quad 0 \le \alpha \le Ce, \qquad y^T\alpha = 0 \tag{7}$$

where e is the vector of all ones, Q is a $N \times N$ semi-positive definite matrix, $Q_{ij} = y_i y_j K(x_i, x_j)$ with K being the kernel function.

This chapter follows [9] and employs the radial basis function (RBF): $k(x_i, x_j) = exp\left\{-\gamma|x_i - x_j|^2\right\}$, where γ and C are hyperparameters to be selected. A series of SVMs with $C = 2^c$ and $\gamma = 2^g$ are implemented. Based on a 10-fold cross-validation, the best parameters are $C = 32$ and $\gamma = 0.25$. The overall classification accuracy turns out to be 67.2% for SVM, which lies between ORL and RF.

Neural Network (NN) The artificial neural network (NN) models are proposed by cognitive scientists to mimic the way that brain processes information. As noted by [32], NN can be viewed as a nonlinear regression model in the following form,

$$f(x, \theta) = \tilde{x}'\alpha + \sum_{s}^{q} G(\tilde{x}'\gamma_s)\beta_s \tag{8}$$

where $\tilde{x} = (1, x')'$, q is a integer representing the number of hidden neurons, and $G(\cdot)$ is a given nonlinear activation function. NN processes information in a hierarchical manner: the signals from an *input node* x_j $(i = 1,\cdots,20)$ are first amplified or attenuated by γ_{js} and arrive at q *hidden* (intermediate) *nodes*. The aggregated signals, in the form of $tildex'\gamma_s$, are then passed to the seven *output nodes* (e.g., the potential rating outcome) by the operation of the activation function $G(\tilde{x}'\gamma_s)$. As in the previous step, information at the hidden node s is amplified or attenuated by β_s. Other than through hidden nodes, signals are also allowed to affect the rating outcome directly through weights α.

For simplicity, this study focuses on a three-layer NN and varies the number of nodes in the hidden layer for training. In particular, 5, 10, 15, 20 hidden nodes are used. For each case, we run the same model with 50 replications to tease out the impact of bad starting values. In terms of the predictive accuracy, we find that the model with five hidden nodes slightly outperforms the rest (57.3, 56.4, 56.3, and 55.4%). In **Table 10**, we report the classification matrix for one of the NN models, with the network structure presented in **Figure 4**.

4.2 Sensitivity analysis

To explore which features are more important than others in predicting ratings, we performed two sensitivity analyses. While the analyses can be applied to any aforementioned ML methods, we decide to focus on RF due to its superior predictive performance.

The first analysis is the variable importance plots (VIP). Loosely speaking, variable importance is the increase in model error when the feature's information is "destroyed." On the left panel of **Figure 5**, we show the impurity-based measure

			Actual Ratings				
Predicted	**Aaa**	**Aa**	**A**	**Baa**	**Ba**	**B**	**C**
Aaa	11	3	3	0	0	0	0
Aa	0	7	5	0	0	0	0
A	26	51	171	73	2	0	0
Baa	0	1	79	319	47	9	0
Ba	0	0	0	19	21	12	0
B	0	0	0	33	33	71	2
C	0	0	0	0	0	0	1
Total	37	62	258	444	103	93	3
Accuracy							60.1%

Table 10.
The classification confusion matrix of NN in holdout sample.

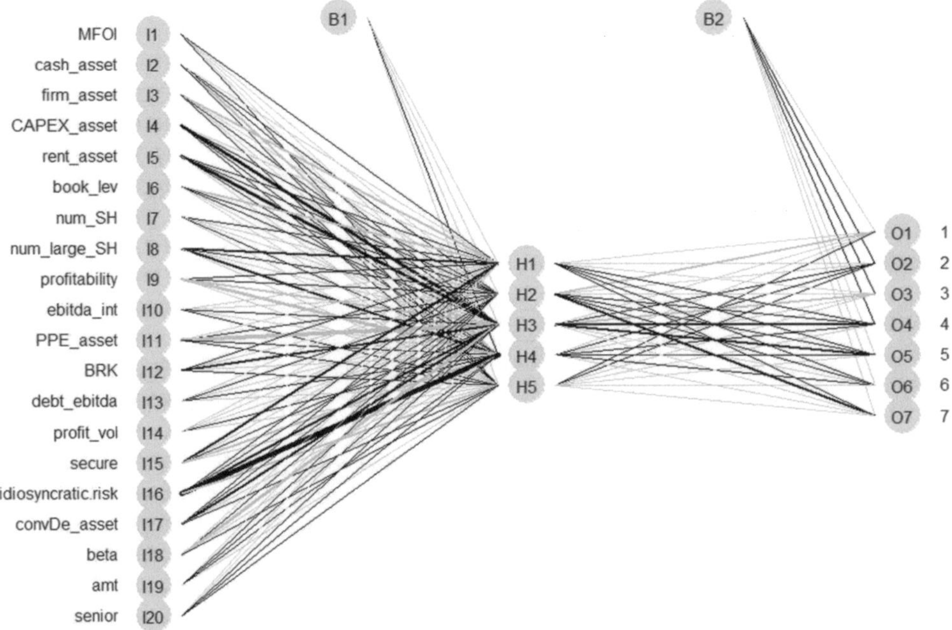

Figure 4.
NN with five hidden nodes (A darker line means a stronger signal).

where we base feature importance on the average total reduction of the loss function for a given feature across all trees. On the right panel, we show the permutation-based importance measure[6]. A feature is "important" if shuffling its values increases the model error, because in this case the model relied on the feature for the prediction.

[6] In the permutation-based approach, the values for each variable are randomly permuted, one at a time, and the accuracy is again computed. The decrease in accuracy as a result of this randomly shuffling of feature values is averaged over all the trees for each predictor [33].

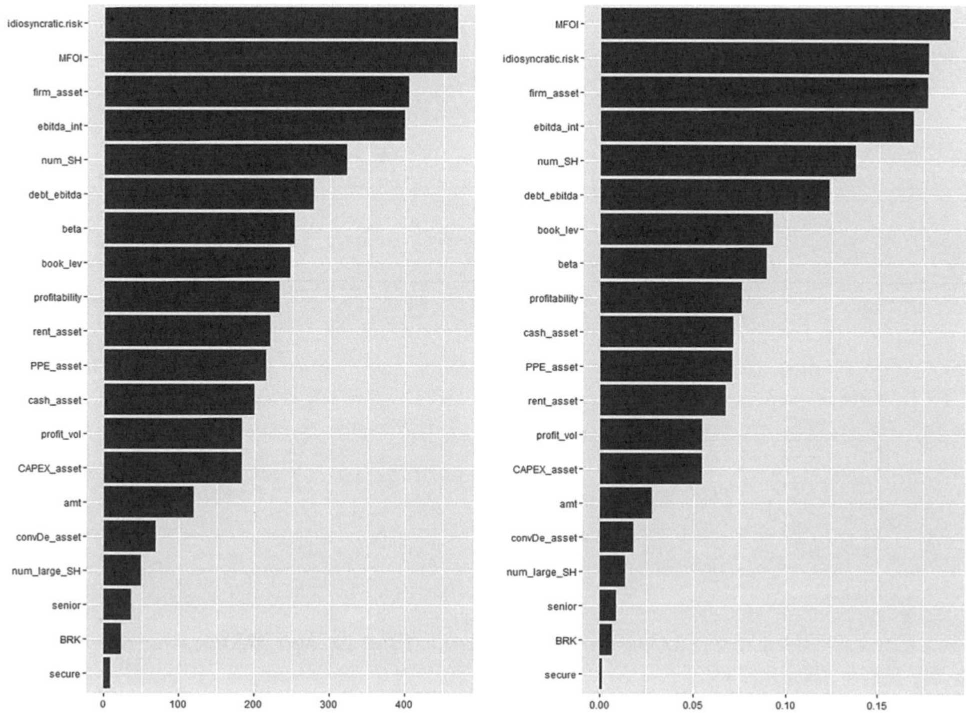

Figure 5.
Variable importance plot of each attribute for the RF model. Note: the figure on the left (right) ranks importance based on the Gini-impurity (permutation).

Both measures consistently identify the two most important attributes to be MFOI and the idiosyncratic risk of the bond issuer's stock. Eliminating the information contained in MFOI, from the permutation-based metric, decreases the predictive accuracy by about 20%.

The second sensitivity analysis is to compute the Partial Dependence (PD) for important attributes. To describe the notion of partial dependence, let $X = \{x_1, x_2, \cdots, x_{20}\}$ represent the set of the predictor variables in the RF model where the prediction function is denoted by $\hat{f}(X)$. The "partial dependence" of x_1, for example, is defined as

$$PD(x_1) = \frac{\partial}{\partial x_1} \mathbf{E}_{x_1}\left[\hat{f}(x_1,\ x_c)\right] = \frac{\partial}{\partial x_1} \int \hat{f}(x_1, x_c) p_c(x_c) dx_c \tag{9}$$

where $X_c = \{x_2, x_3, \cdots, x_{20}\}$ denote the other predictors and $p_c(x_c)$ is the marginal probability density of $x_c : p_c(x_c) = \int p(X) dx_c$. This quantity, which resembles a marginal effect, can be estimated from a set of training data by

$$\hat{PD}(x_1) = \frac{1}{n} \sum_i \frac{\partial}{\partial x_1} \hat{f}(x_1, x_{c,i}) \tag{10}$$

where $x_{c,i}$ are the values of x_c that occur in the training sample; that is, we average out the effects of all the other predictors in the model. In **Figure 6**, we report the PDs

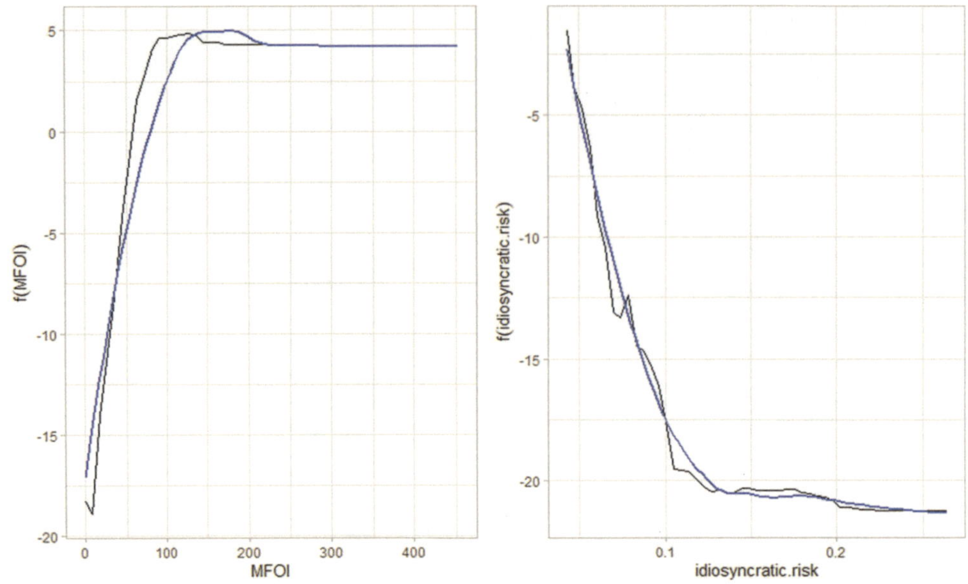

Figure 6.
Partial dependence plot for MFOI and idiosyncratic risk from the RF model. Note: The black line depicts the PD at specific values of MFOI/idiosyncratic risk. The blue line is the fitted value.

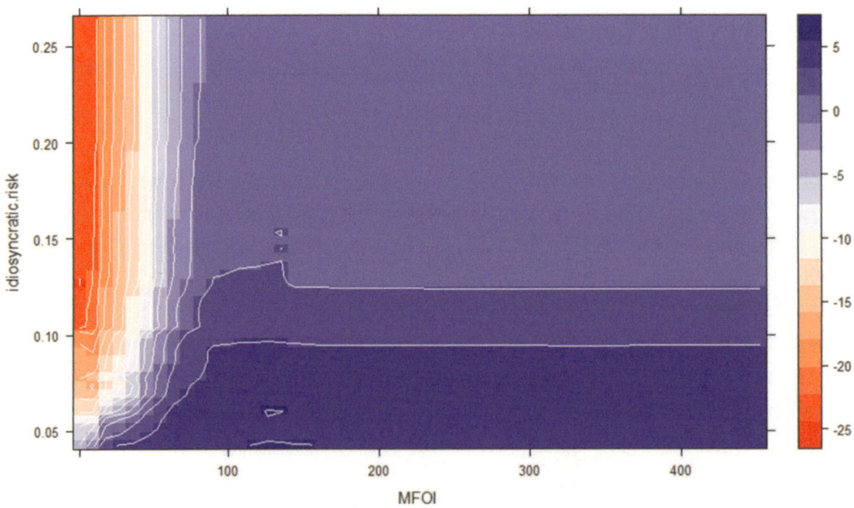

Figure 7.
Joint partial dependence plot for MFOI and idiosyncratic risk.

for MFOI and idiosyncratic risk separately. From the left panel, a lower value of MFOI has a negative impact on the rating outcome. As MFOI goes above 50, it starts to affect the rating in a positive way (a higher degree of connectedness between Moody and the issuer firm, as measured by MFOI, translates to a higher predicted rating). The positive impact of MFOI increases with the level of MFOI and plateaues as MFOI goes above 150, which is about the 99 percentile of its distribution. Conversely, we see that a larger idiosyncratic risk has a more deteriorating impact on ratings. Both patterns are economically sounding. **Figure** 7 represents the joint PD for MFOI and idiosyncratic risk. The negative impact of idiosyncratic risk is only pronounced when MFOI is low.

4.3 Discussion

The main message emerged from our empirical exercise is that conflicts of interest, as measured by bond issuer's connection with Moody's shareholders, have a strong predictive power in the credit rating outcome. This observation is consistent with several previous studies. [16] found that Moody's has been assigning more favorable ratings (relative to that of S&P's) to issuers related to its two largest shareholders—Berkshire Hathaway and Davis Selected Advisors. [23, 34] showed that such bias is more universal and apply to issuers associated with any large shareholders of Moody's.

Although cross-ownership has been recognized in the literature as a important driver of credit ratings, it has not been explicitly considered as a predictor variable in any prior studies that focus on prediction. This study complements the above by confirming that cross-ownership can be utilized to increase the predictability of credit ratings.

5. Conclusions

In this chapter, we employ six machine learning methods to predict bond ratings from a sample of US public firms. Other than the financial ratios employed by previous studies, this chapter expands the feature sets to include equity risk measures and the bond issuer's cross-ownership relation with the rating agency. Inclusion of the latter source of information is unprecedented.

Several observations/conclusions emerge from the analysis. (1) Ensemble methods, including the Random Forest, Bagged Decision Trees, and Gradient Boosting Machines, generally outperform the ML methods with a single classifier. (2) Among the three ensemble methods, random forest shows a significantly better performance than the other (correctly predicting 5% more bonds than bagging and 10% more bonds than boosting). (3) Sensitivity analyses reveals the firm's idiosyncratic risk and cross-ownership relation with the rating agency as the two most important attributes in predicting ratings.

Author details

Yixiao Jiang†
Economics, Christopher Newport University, Newport News, USA

*Address all correspondence to: yixiao.jiang@cnu.edu

† This research is supported by the Christopher Newport University Faculty Development Fund.

References

[1] Altman EI. Financial ratios, discriminant analysis and the prediction of corporate bankruptcy. The Journal of Finance. 1968;**23**(4):589-609

[2] Horrigan JO. The determination of long-term credit standing with financial ratios. Journal of Accounting Research. 1966:44-62

[3] Kaplan RS, Urwitz G. Statistical models of bond ratings: A methodological inquiry. Journal of Business. 1979:231-261

[4] Pinches GE, Mingo KA. A multivariate analysis of industrial bond ratings. The Journal of Finance. 1973; **28**(1):1-18

[5] West RR. An alternative approach to predicting corporate bond ratings. Journal of Accounting Research. 1970: 118-125

[6] Bellotti T, Matousek R, Stewart C. A note comparing support vector machines and ordered choice models' predictions of international banks' ratings. Decision Support Systems. 2011;**51**(3):682-687

[7] Huang Z, Chen H, Hsu C-J, Chen W-H, Soushan W. Credit rating analysis with support vector machines and neural networks: a market comparative study. Decision Support Systems. 2004;**37**(4): 543-558

[8] Kumar K, Bhattacharya S. Artificial neural network vs linear discriminant analysis in credit ratings forecast. Review of Accounting and Finance. 2006;**5**(3):216-227

[9] Lee Y-C. Application of support vector machines to corporate credit rating prediction. Expert Systems with Applications. 2007;**33**(1):67-74

[10] Sermpinis G, Tsoukas S, Zhang P. Modelling market implied ratings using lasso variable selection techniques. Journal of Empirical Finance. 2018;**48**: 19-35

[11] Yeh C-C, Lin F, Hsu C-Y. A hybrid kmv model, random forests and rough set theory approach for credit rating. Knowledge-Based Systems. 2012;**33**: 166-172

[12] Bauer E, Kohavi R. An empirical comparison of voting classification algorithms: Bagging, boosting, and variants. Machine Learning. 1999;**36**(1): 105-139

[13] Drucker H, et al. Boosting and other machine learning algorithms. In: Machine Learning Proceedings 1994. MA, USA: Morgan Kaufmann; 1994. pp. 53-61

[14] Freund Y, Schapire RE, et al. Experiments with a new boosting algorithm. In: ICML. Vol. 96. Citeseer; 1996. pp. 148-156

[15] Jiang Y. Semiparametric estimation of a corporate bond rating model. Econometrics. 2021;**9**(2):23

[16] Kedia S, Rajgopal S, Zhou XA. Large shareholders and credit ratings. Journal of Financial Economics. 2017;**124**(3): 632-653

[17] Baghai R, Becker B. Non-rating revenue and conflicts of interest. Swedish House of Finance Research Paper, (15-06). 2016

[18] Cornaggia J, Cornaggia KJ, Xia H. Revolving doors on wall street. Journal of Financial Economics. 2016;**120**(2): 400-419

[19] Boubaker S, Sami H. Multiple large shareholders and earnings informativeness. Review of Accounting and Finance. 2011

[20] Khoshgoftaar TM, Golawala M, Van Hulse J. An empirical study of learning from imbalanced data using random forest. In 19th IEEE International Conference on Tools with Artificial Intelligence (ICTAI 2007). IEEE. Vol. 2. 2007. pp. 310–317

[21] Muchlinski D, Siroky D, He J, Kocher M. Comparing random forest with logistic regression for predicting class-imbalanced civil war onset data. Political Analysis. 2016:87-103

[22] Baghai RP, Servaes H, Tamayo A. Have rating agencies become more conservative? Implications for capital structure and debt pricing. The Journal of Finance. 2014;**69**(5):1961-2005

[23] Jiang Y. Credit ratings, financial ratios, and equity risk: A decomposition analysis based on moody's, standard & poor's and fitch's ratings. Finance Research Letters. 2021:-102512

[24] Breiman L. Bagging predictors. Machine Learning. 1996;**24**(2):123-140

[25] Breiman L. Random forests. Machine Learning. 2001;**45**(1):5-32

[26] Ho TK. Random decision forests. In: Proceedings of 3rd International Conference on Document Analysis and Recognition. IEEE. Vol. 1, 1995. pp. 278–282

[27] Amit Y, Geman D. Shape quantization and recognition with randomized trees. Neural Computation. 1997;**9**(7):1545-1588

[28] Hastie T, Tibshirani R, Friedman J. The Elements of Statistical Learnin. Cited on 2009. p. 33

[29] Madeh Piryonesi S, El-Diraby TE. Using machine learning to examine impact of type of performance indicator on flexible pavement deterioration modeling. Journal of Infrastructure Systems. 2021;**27**(2):04021005

[30] Opitz D, Maclin R. Popular ensemble methods: An empirical study. Journal of Artificial Intelligence Research. 1999;**11**: 169-198

[31] Vapnik VN. An overview of statistical learning theory. IEEE Transactions on Neural Networks. 1999; **10**(5):988-999

[32] Swanson NR, White H. A model-selection approach to assessing the information in the term structure using linear models and artificial neural networks. Journal of Business & Economic Statistics. 1995;**13**(3):265-275

[33] Boehmke B, Greenwell BM. Hands-on Machine Learning with R. New York, USA: CRC Press; 2019

[34] Gu Z, Jiang Y, Yang S. Estimating unobserved soft adjustment in bond rating models: Before and after the dodd-frank act. Available at SSRN 3277328. 2018

Chapter 3

Forecasting Weekly Shipments of Hass Avocados from Mexico to the United States Using Econometric and Vector Autoregression Models

Oral Capps

Abstract

Domestic production cannot meet the U.S. demand for avocados, satisfying only 10% of the national demand. Due to year-round production and longer shelf-life, the Hass variety of avocados accounts for about 85% of avocados consumed in the United States and roughly 95% of total avocado imports, primarily from Mexico. Using weekly data over the period July 3, 2011, to October 24, 2021, econometric and vector autoregression models are estimated regarding the seven main shipment sizes of Hass avocados from Mexico to the United States. Both types of models discern the impacts of inflation-adjusted and exchange-rate adjusted prices per box as well as U.S. disposable income, holidays and events, and seasonality on the level of Hass avocado shipments by size. In general, these impacts are robust across the respective models by shipment size. These types of models also mimic the variability in the level of shipments by size quite well based on goodness-of-fit metrics. Based on absolute percent error, these models provide reasonably accurate forecasts of the level of Hass avocado shipments from Mexico by size associated with a time horizon of 13 weeks. But neither type of models provides better forecast performance universally across all avocado shipment sizes.

Keywords: Hass avocado shipments from Mexico, econometric models, vector autoregression (VAR) models, forecasts, and forecast accuracy

1. Introduction

> *"Self-styled "prophets" who mislead us should be reminded that among the ancient Scythians, when prophets predicted things that failed to come true, they were laid, shackled hand and foot, on a little cart filled with heather and drawn by oxen, on which they were burned to death"-Unknown. "In science and in real economic life, it is terribly important not to be wrong much" [1].*

Avocado is the fruit of the avocado tree, scientifically known as *Persea Americana*. This fruit is sought after because of its high nutrient value and often is added to various dishes due to its appealing flavor and rich texture. Avocado is the main

ingredient in guacamole. The avocado has become an incredibly popular food among health-conscious individuals, often referred to as a superfood [2]. Per capita consumption of fresh avocados has increased markedly from 2.21 pounds in 2000 to 9.05 pounds in 2020 [3]. This surge in per capita consumption in roughly 20 years is slightly more than 300%.

In the United States, three commercial avocado regions are evident: Southern California, Florida, and Hawaii. Among these three areas, California produces the majority of the avocados followed by Florida and Hawaii. However, domestic production cannot meet the U.S. demand for avocados, satisfying only 10% of the national demand for avocados [4]. Due to year-round production and longer shelf-life, the Hass variety of avocados is the dominant and the most popular commercial type. Hass avocados account for about 85% of avocados consumed in the United States and roughly 95% of total avocado imports, primarily from Mexico, the major producer of avocados in the world [5, 6]. As such, we concentrate solely on the demand for Hass avocados.

2. Objectives

The objectives of this investigation are twofold: (1) to develop econometric and vector autoregression (VAR) models associated with the seven main shipment sizes of Hass avocados from Mexico to the United States; and (2) to provide ex-post forecasts over a period of 13 weeks out-of-sample. The main purpose of this investigation is to determine which class of models yields the better forecasts of weekly shipments. This analysis is of utmost importance to the Mexican Hass Avocado Importer Association (MHAIA) as well as stakeholders in the avocado industry in general.

The historical data used to estimate the respective models span the period with the week ending July 3, 2011, to the week ending October 24, 2021, a total of 539 observations. Based on these model specifications, we derive ex-post weekly forecasts over the week ending October 31, 2021, to the week ending January 23, 2022. Because the forecasts were generated over a period for which we have actual historical data, we are in position to determine their accuracy. Metrics used to determine forecast accuracy typically include root mean squared error (RMSE), mean absolute error (MAE), and mean absolute percent error (MAPE) [1, 7–9]. Because the levels of avocado shipments are not the same across the respective sizes, in this analysis, attention is centered exclusively on MAPE. With MAPE, forecast accuracy is devoid of units of measurement.

3. Methodology

The econometric models consider the direct effects of specific market variables on weekly shipment levels of Hass avocados to the United States by size. Seven sizes (32, 36, 40, 48, 60, 70, and 84) of Hass avocados historically have accounted for close to 99% of all shipments since July 2011. The respective sizes refer to the number of avocados per box. The seven econometric models are single-equation relationships which account for seasonality, changes in real U.S. disposable personal income, changes in the Mexican peso to U.S. dollar exchange rate, changes in the real price per box of avocados shipped, inertia of shipments (a one-period lag of shipments), and qualitative events such as Cinco de Mayo, the Super Bowl, holidays (July 4/

Independence Day, Thanksgiving, and Christmas), beginning of the month, end of the month, end of the year, the pandemic, and work stoppages.

Mathematically, the econometric model specification for this analysis is as follows:

$$\ln \mathbf{Y}_{it} = \boldsymbol{\beta}' \ln \mathbf{X}_{it} + \boldsymbol{\alpha}' \boldsymbol{Z}_{it} + \varepsilon_{it}, i = 1,2, \dots ,N, t = 1,2, \dots ,T \qquad (1)$$

where $\mathbf{lnY_{it}}$ is the logarithmic transformation of shipments of Hass avocados from Mexico to the United States by size i at time t, $\mathbf{lnX_{it}}$ is a column vector of logarithmic transformations of the continuous explanatory variables for size i in time t. $\mathbf{Z_{it}}$ corresponds to additional explanatory variables, namely indicator variables which correspond to the previously mentioned qualitative events. $\boldsymbol{\alpha}'$ and $\boldsymbol{\beta}'$ are the conformable vectors of parameters to be estimated, and $\boldsymbol{\varepsilon}_{\mathbf{it}}$ is a column vector of error terms. As a result of the use of logarithmic transformations, $\boldsymbol{\beta}'$ also represents the elasticities associated with the continuous explanatory variables.

According to Sims [10], one may consider equation (1) as multiple economic time series where lags (to be determined from the data and *a priori* knowledge) of each variable are allowed to affect the current position of each series. The general statement of the vector autoregressive model (VAR) is given as:

$$x_t = \sum_{k=1}^{K} \alpha(k) x_{t-k} + e_t, \qquad (2)$$

where $\alpha(k)$ is an autoregressive matrix of dimension (nxn) at lag k which connects x_t and $x_{t\text{-}k}$, the vector of endogenous variables and lagged endogenous variables, n represents the number of endogenous variables included in the model, and e_t is a vector residual term of dimension (nx1). Most of the autoregressive parameters $\alpha(k)$ are equal to zero and K is the maximum lag based on model selection criteria such as the Akaike, Schwarz, and Hannan-Quinn information criteria (AIC, SIC, and HQC). In this analysis, the endogenous variables included in the VAR are the logarithmic transformation of shipments of Hass avocados from Mexico to the United States by size at time t. Hence, like the econometric models, the VAR consists of seven equations. In the VAR, we also include as exogenous variables real U.S. disposable personal income, the Mexican peso to U.S. dollar exchange rate, and the real price per box of avocados shipped as well as the qualitative variables previously described. Hence this specification technically is a structural vector autoregression model (SVAR).

Unit root tests, based on the use of Augmented Dickey-Fuller (ADF) tests, were conducted prior to the estimation of the VAR. In all cases, the respective endogenous variables are stationary or I(0). Thus, the appropriate model is a VAR in levels specification. Because the respective endogenous variables are stationary in levels, the examination of co-integration is superfluous.

To determine whether estimated coefficients are significantly different from zero, we adopt a level of significance of 0.10 for the econometric models and for the VAR model. This choice of the level of significance is conservative in terms of determining the key factors associated with shipments of Hass avocados from Mexico, especially given the number of weekly observations in this analysis.

3.1 Historical Avocado Shipments by Size

Historical weekly avocado shipments, the dependent variables in this investigation, in metric tons by size over the period July 3, 2011, to October 24, 2021, are shown

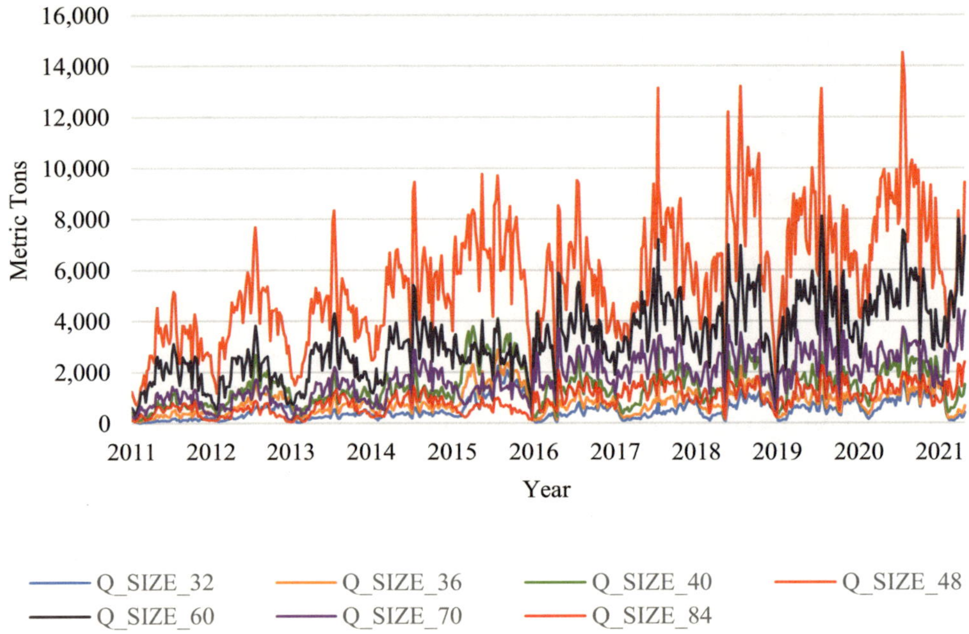

Figure 1.
Weekly Shipments of Hass Avocados from Mexico to the United States by Size, July 3, 2011, to October 24, 2021. Source: Mexican Hass Importer Association [11] and the Hass Avocado Board [12].

in **Figure 1**. Shipments have increased over this period in all size classes, although they fluctuate noticeably from week to week. As well, the weekly deviations can be quite severe. Additionally, the avocado shipments of each size show definite seasonal patterns. In general, shipments for most sizes are seasonally lowest in July when the Normal and Marzeña harvests wind down and when the Loca and Aventajada harvests begin. Shipments tend to hit a peak each year in January in preparation for the Super Bowl, historically the largest avocado consuming season in the United States.

The descriptive statistics associated the dependent variables associated with the respective class of models is exhibited in **Table 1**. The label Q_SIZE_ refers to the shipment size measured in metric tons. On average, the weekly shipments vary from 515.53 metric tons (size 32) to 5,631.28 metric tons (size 48). The average share sizes of the respective weekly shipments over the 539 weekly periods are 3.46 percent for size 32; 5.79 percent for size 36; 9.99 percent for size 40; 39.61 percent for size 48; 22.83 percent for size 60; 12.19 percent for size 70; and 6.12 percent for size 84. Consequently, the two main sizes of weekly Hass avocado shipments are 48 and 60, combining for slightly more than 60 percent of total avocado shipments from Mexico to the United States.

4. Empirical results

Due to space limitations, the estimated parameters, standard errors, and p-values of the econometric models and the vector autoregression model are not reported. This information however is available from the author upon request.

Descriptive statistic	Q_SIZE_32	Q_SIZE_36	Q_SIZE_40	Q_SIZE_48	Q_SIZE_60	Q_SIZE_70	Q_SIZE_84
Mean	515.53	827.13	1,432.76	5,631.28	3,258.39	1,772.76	900.99
Median	413.02	747.75	1 345.58	5,420.38	3,074.43	1,689.01	845.76
Maximum	2,239.92	2875.40	4 101.05	14,523.68	8,103.01	4,454.53	2,375.21
Minimum	9.23	58.27	118.68	723.03	329.01	128.68	50.26
Std. Dev	399.08	491.78	751.86	2,366.38	1,460.29	887.89	497.03

Table 1.
Descriptive Statistics of the Weekly Shipments of Hass Avocados from Mexico to the United States by Size in Metric Tons, July 3, 2011, to October 24, 2021. Source: Calculations by the author.

Each of the respective econometric models is estimated by ordinary least squares (OLS) using the software packages EVIEWS 11.0.[1] The VAR model is estimated by seemingly unrelated regression (SUR) using the software package EVIEWS 11.0. Based on model selection criteria, the optimal lag length chosen in the VAR model is 1.

Both classes of models fit the historical weekly shipments well based on their goodness-of-fit (R^2 and adjusted R^2) statistics. The respective econometric models explain between 85% and 93% of the weekly variability of avocado shipments, while the respective VAR model explains between 86% and 94% of the weekly variability of avocado shipments. Given the variability inherent in weekly shipments, simply put, the econometric models and the VAR model replicate the behavior of historical shipments quite well.

The continuous explanatory variables include lags of the logarithmic transformations of the avocado shipments. The econometric models include only the lag of the dependent variable in a particular equation, but the VAR model includes lags of all dependent variables in all equations. Both sets of models include the logarithmic transformation of real (inflation-adjusted) disposable income in the United States multiplied by the Mexico peso to U.S. dollar exchange rate and the logarithmic transformation of inflation-adjusted prices per box (in U.S. dollars) multiplied by the Mexican peso to U.S. dollar exchange rate. Consequently, the coefficients associated with inflation- and exchange-rate-adjusted disposable personal income and prices per box are elasticities.

Indicator variables associated with each calendar month are included to account for seasonality. The base or reference category is the month of July. As well, indicator variables are included to account for holidays, work stoppages, the beginning and ending of each month, the end of the calendar year, and the pandemic. The qualitative variable associated with the pandemic is equal to 1 beginning March 8, 2020, through October 24, 2021, and 0 otherwise. Finally, influential data points (outliers and leverage points) based on R-student statistics and hat diagonal elements also are accounted for with the use of indicator variables [14].

Impulse responses provide the impact of a *one-time* change in the "impulse variable" on the "response" variable over the course of several periods. In this analysis, the impulse variable is a *particular* endogenous variable in the system that pertains to the magnitude of Hass avocado shipments from Mexico of a *certain* size; the response variable refers to the magnitudes of any of the other remaining Hass avocado shipments from Mexico of other sizes. The number of periods to consider for the impulse-response functions is arbitrary. In this analysis, 13 weeks (one quarter) are considered. The impulse response functions associated with the VAR analysis are exhibited in **Figure 2**.

The variance decomposition of a particular endogenous variable indicates the percentage of its forecast error variance explained by shocks attributed to other endogenous variables in the system. Again, the number of periods to consider is arbitrary. Like the situation for the impulse response functions, 13 weeks (one quarter) are considered. For any period, the percentages associated with the respective endogenous variables must sum to 1. The variance decompositions associated with the VAR analysis are exhibited in **Figure 3**.

Most of the forecast error variance (between 81 and 99 percent) associated with Hass avocados of size 32 is explained by itself. The forecast error variance associated

[1] The models also were estimated using seemingly unrelated regression [13]. But the statistical gains in efficiency were negligible. Consequently, only the OLS results are discussed.

with Hass avocados of size 36 is explained by the volume of Hass avocados of size 32 (between 67 and 73 percent) and size 36 (between 19 and 28 percent). The forecast error variance associated with Hass avocados of size 40 is attributed to the volume of Hass avocados of size 32 (between 60 and 69 percent), size 36 (between 13 and 15 percent), and size 40 (between 17 and 21 percent). The forecast error variance associated with Hass avocados of size 48 is explained by the volume of Hass avocados of size 32 (between 52 and 56 percent), size 36 (between 13 and 16 percent), and size 48 (between 20 and 22 percent). The forecast error variance associated with Hass

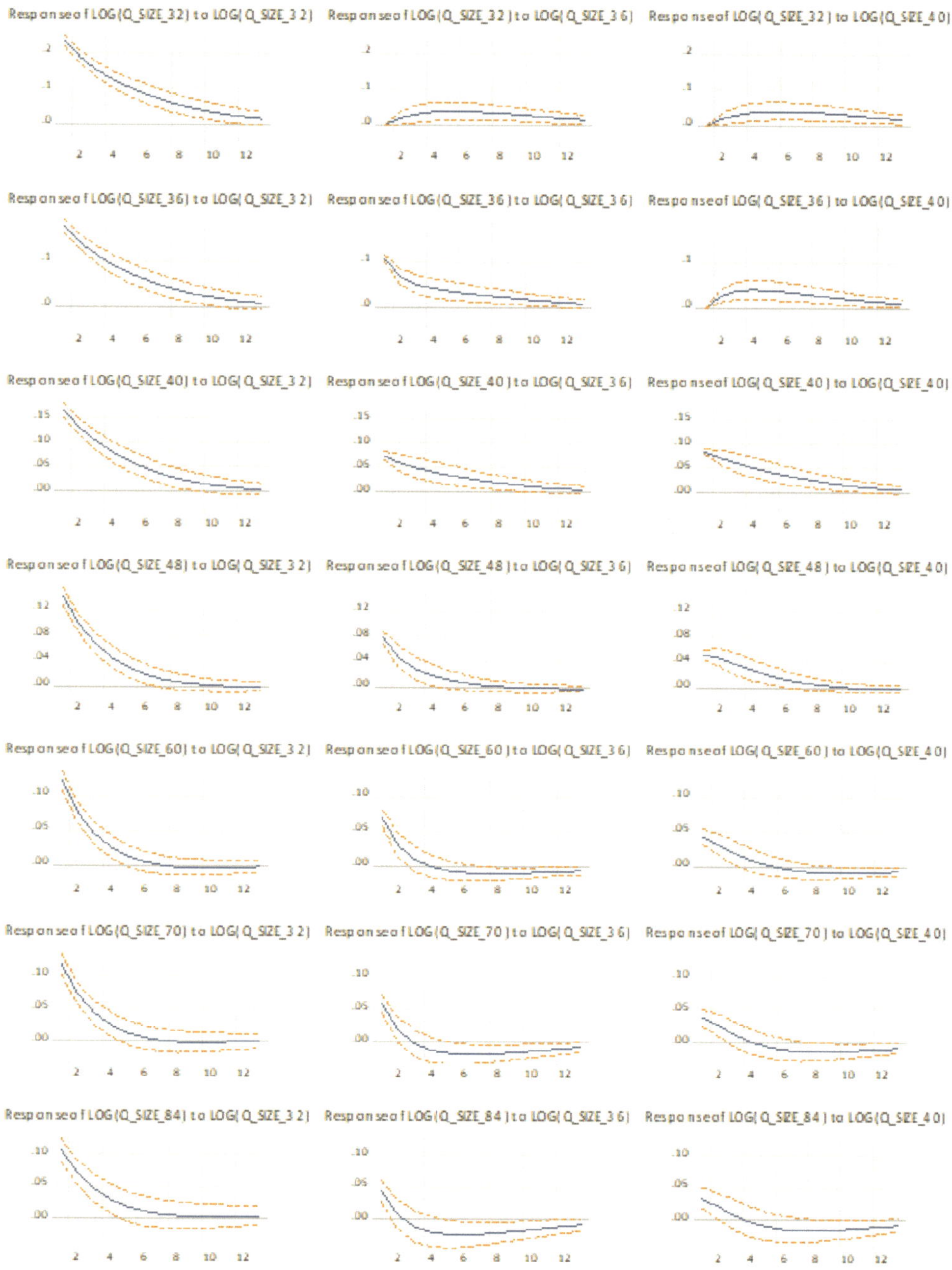

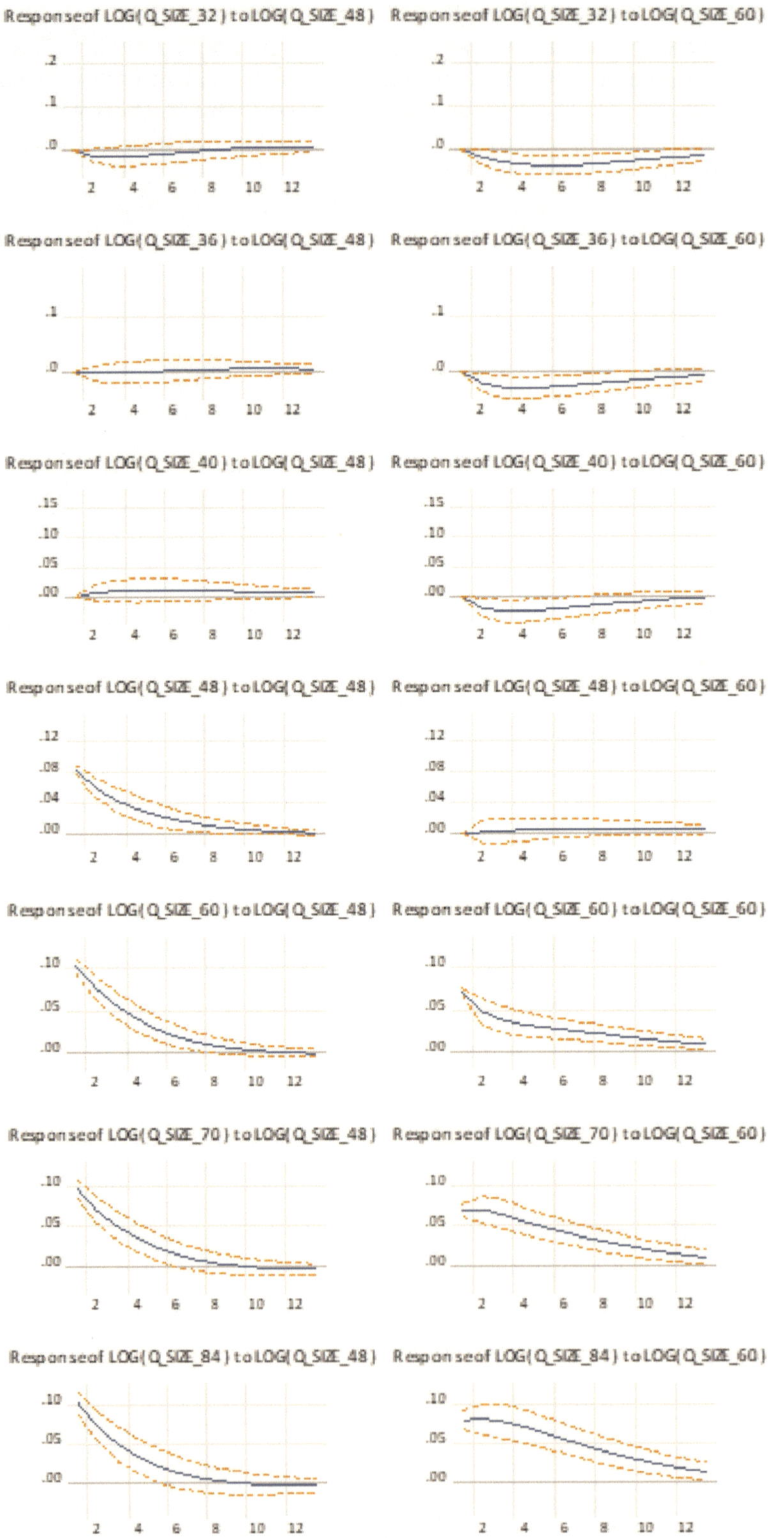
Response of LOG(Q_SIZE_32) to LOG(Q_SIZE_48)
Response of LOG(Q_SIZE_32) to LOG(Q_SIZE_60)
Response of LOG(Q_SIZE_36) to LOG(Q_SIZE_48)
Response of LOG(Q_SIZE_36) to LOG(Q_SIZE_60)
Response of LOG(Q_SIZE_40) to LOG(Q_SIZE_48)
Response of LOG(Q_SIZE_40) to LOG(Q_SIZE_60)
Response of LOG(Q_SIZE_48) to LOG(Q_SIZE_48)
Response of LOG(Q_SIZE_48) to LOG(Q_SIZE_60)
Response of LOG(Q_SIZE_60) to LOG(Q_SIZE_48)
Response of LOG(Q_SIZE_60) to LOG(Q_SIZE_60)
Response of LOG(Q_SIZE_70) to LOG(Q_SIZE_48)
Response of LOG(Q_SIZE_70) to LOG(Q_SIZE_60)
Response of LOG(Q_SIZE_84) to LOG(Q_SIZE_48)
Response of LOG(Q_SIZE_84) to LOG(Q_SIZE_60)

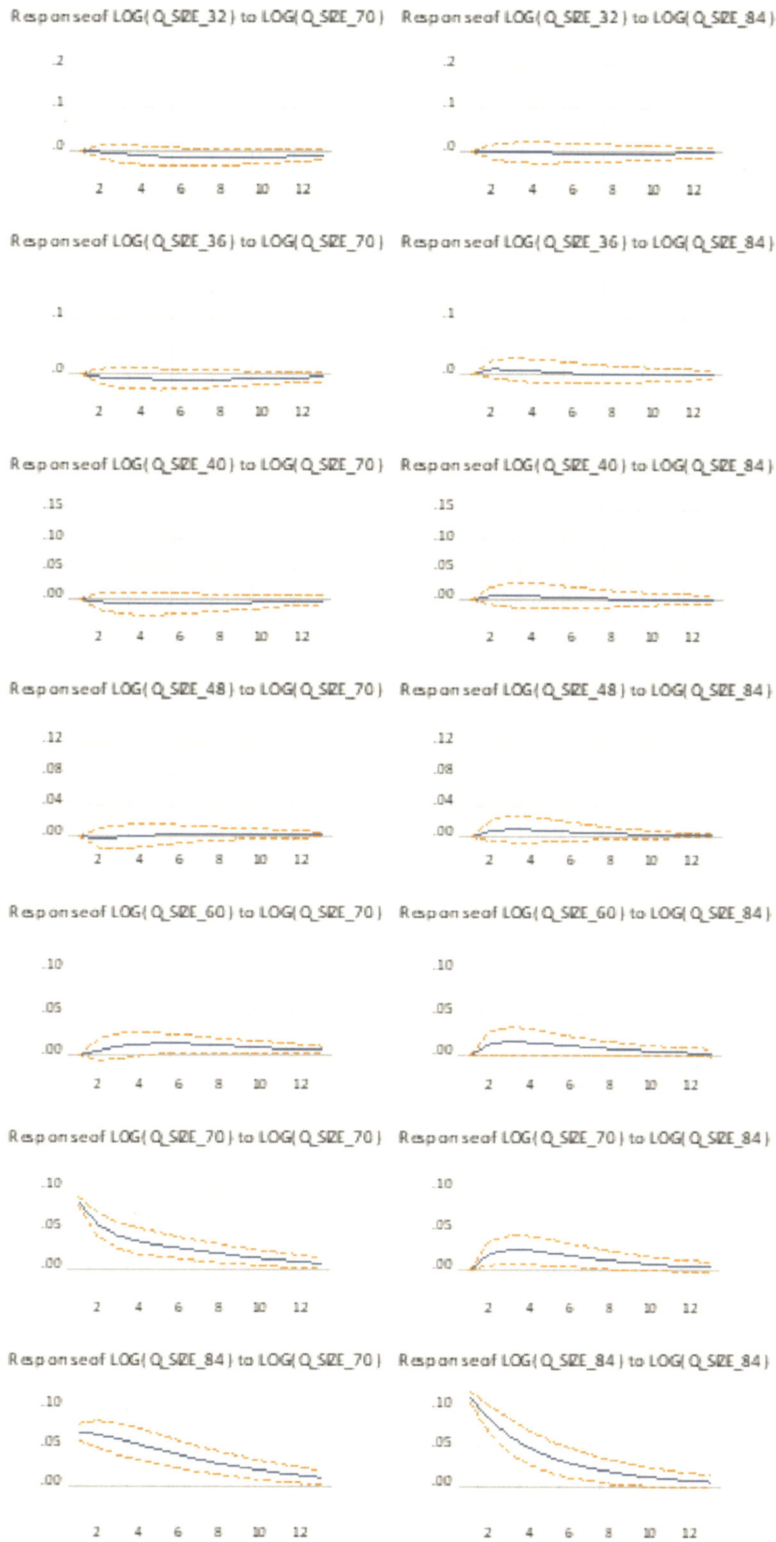

Figure 2.
Impulse Response Functions Associated with the VAR Analysis.

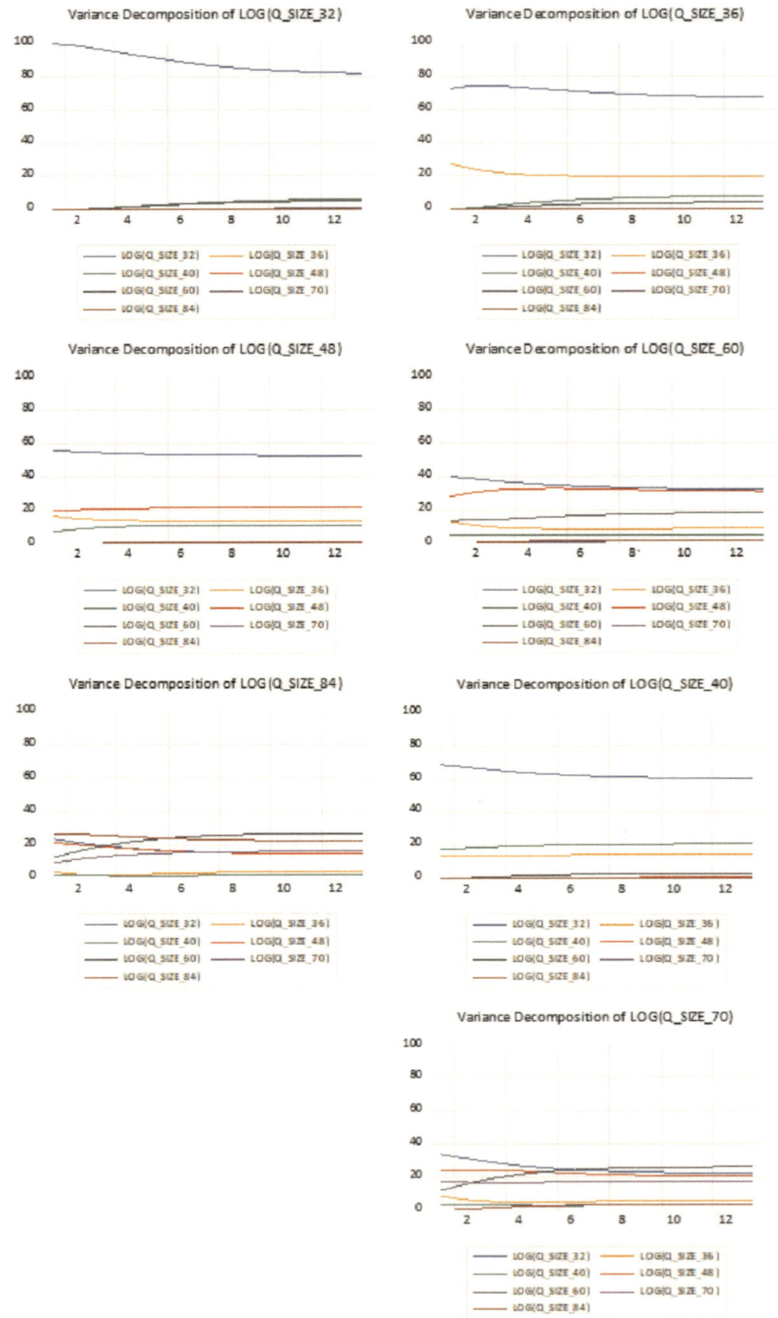

Figure 3.
Variance Decompositions Associated with the VAR analysis.

avocados of size 60 is attributed to the volume of Hass avocados of size 32 (between 32 and 40 percent), size 48 (between 28 and 33 percent), and size 60 (between 14 and 18 percent). The forecast error variance associated with Hass avocados of size 70 is explained by the volume of Hass avocados of size 32 (between 22 and 32 percent), size 48 (between 20 and 24 percent), size 60 (between 12 and 26 percent), and size 70 (roughly 17 percent). Finally, the forecast error variance associated with Hass avocados of size 84 is attributed to the volume of Hass avocados of size 32 (between 15 and 23 percent), size 48 (between 14 and 21 percent), size 60 (between 13 and 27 percent), size 70 (between 9 and 17 percent), and size 84 (between 22 and 27 percent).

Seasonal troughs are evident in July for all sizes in both the econometric models and the VAR model0. Additionally, avocado shipments from Mexico are higher in January, March, April, September, October, November, and December relative to July for all sizes.

The effects of exchange rate and inflation are embedded in the U.S. dollar per box price. For the econometric models, the own-price elasticity (responsiveness) of the respective sizes are as follows: size 32, -0.2081; size 36, -0.1864; size 40, -0.1490; and size 48, -0.1156. The own-price elasticities monotonically decrease in size (in absolute value) with increases in box size. No price responsiveness is evident for shipments of sizes 60, 70 and 84. Consequently, the prices per box associated with these shipment sizes were dropped from those econometric models. The VAR model, unlike the econometric models, includes prices per box for all sizes of avocado shipments. But not all coefficients associated with the respective prices are significantly different from zero. Non-significant coefficients regarding prices per box were dropped in the VAR model. Only 13 of the 49 coefficients associated with prices are significantly different from zero in the VAR model. The prices of sizes 40, 48, 60, and 70 impact avocado shipments of size 32. The prices of sizes 40 and 48 affect avocado shipments of size 36. The price of size 32 impacts avocado shipments of size 40, while the prices of sizes 40 and 84 impact avocado shipments of size 48. Prices of the respective box sizes do not affect avocado shipments of size 60. The prices of sizes 60 and 70 impact avocado shipments of size 70, and the prices of sizes 60 and 84 impact avocado shipments of size 84. The statistically significant price elasticities in the VAR model range from -0.4169 to -0.4985. Bottom line, for both the econometric and VAR models, Hass avocado shipments from Mexico to the United States are not sensitive to inflation-adjusted and exchange-rate adjusted prices per box.

On the other hand, avocado shipments are responsive to changes in U.S disposable personal income, adjusted for inflation and exchange rates. The income elasticity of the respective sizes from the econometric models are as follows: size, 32 0.4162; size 36, 0.3489; size 40, 0.3000; size 48, 0.4172; size 60, 0.3736; size 70, 0.3772; and size 84, 0.2613. The income elasticities of the respective sizes from the VAR model are as follows: size, 32 0.3995; size 36, 0.3639; size 40, 0.3475; size 48, 0.4001; size 60, 0.3649; size 70, 04142; and size 84, 0.2733. Consequently, the estimates of the respective income elasticities are robust across the econometric and VAR models.

Further, in the econometric models, all estimated coefficients associated with the lagged dependent variables are not only positive but also between 0 and 1. This finding also is evident in the VAR model concerning the lag of the dependent variable in question. Hence, this result confirms inertia or persistence in weekly shipments by size of Hass avocados from Mexico to the United States across the econometric and VAR models.

That said, the VAR model, unlike the econometric models, includes one-period lags for all sizes of avocado shipments. But like the situation for prices per box, not all coefficients associated with the respective lags are significantly different from zero. Non-significant coefficients regarding lags of the dependent variables were dropped in the VAR model. Only 29 of the 49 coefficients associated with lags are significantly different from zero in the VAR model.

We consider holiday/calendar events associated with The Super Bowl, Cinco de Mayo, July 4 (Independence Day), Thanksgiving, and Christmas as potential determinants of avocado shipments from Mexico. Importantly, we recognize that lags occur with respect to these holiday/calendar events. As such, we do not consider contemporaneous impacts of the respective holiday/calendar events, but we allow the lags associated with these events to vary from one to four weeks. Subsequently, we choose the optimal lag based on the model selection criteria once again. For The Super Bowl, the optimal lag length is three weeks across all shipment sizes; for Cinco de Mayo, Thanksgiving, and Christmas, the optimal lag length is two weeks across all shipment sizes. The lag length for Independence Day varies from one to four weeks depending on the shipment size in the econometric models. Based on model selection criteria, the lag length for Independence Day is the same (two weeks) across all shipment sizes in the VAR model.

The Super Bowl and the Christmas holiday season have substantial impacts on avocado shipments of all sizes over the historical period of analysis. For the econometric models, the Super Bowl boosts avocado shipments during the three weeks leading up to that event by 26.70 percent (size 70) to 42.61 percent (size 32). For the VAR model, the Super Bowl boosts avocado shipments during the three weeks leading up to that event by 25.90 percent (size 70) to 40.92 percent (size 32). For the two weeks leading up to Christmas, avocado shipments increase from 32.49 percent (size 84) to 53.29 percent (size 36) based on the econometric models. For the two weeks leading up to Christmas, avocado shipments increase from 24.88 percent (size 84) to 48.96 percent (size 36) based on the VAR model.

The Cinco de Mayo, Thanksgiving, and Independence Day holidays deliver much smaller lifts to weekly avocado shipments. For the two weeks leading up to Cinco de Mayo, this lift varies from 6.55 percent (size 40) to 12.92 percent (size 32) in the econometric models and from 6.72 percent to 13.47 percent (size 32) in the VAR model; for the two weeks leading up to Thanksgiving, this lift ranges from 4.23 percent (size 32) to 8.99 percent (size 70) in the econometric models and from 1.90 percent (size 32) to 9.08 percent (size 70) in the VAR model; and for the weeks leading up to Independence Day, this lift varies from 2.71 percent (size 48) to 17.08 percent (size 84) in the econometric models and from 2.63 percent (size 48) to 13.84 percent (size 84) in the VAR model.

Based on the econometric models, work stoppages diminish avocado shipments from 20.95 percent (size 70) to 37.19 percent (size 32); based on the VAR model, work stoppages diminish avocado shipments from 23.24 percent (size 70) to 32.25 percent (size 32). Based on the econometric models, avocado shipments at the end of each calendar year are lower from 19.82 percent (size 32) to 23.73 percent (size 48) on average. Based on the VAR model, avocado shipments at the end of each calendar year are lower from 18.49 percent (size 32) to 24.20 percent (size 60) on average. At the beginning of each month avocado shipments are lower by 3.79 percent (size 84) to 8.94 percent (size 60) on average based on the econometric models. At the beginning of each month avocado shipments are lower by 4.98 percent (size 84) to 8.38 percent (size 60) on average based on the VAR model. At the end of each month avocado shipments are lower by 4.82 percent (size 84) to 8.33 percent (size 40) on average in the econometric models. At the end of each month avocado shipments are lower by 4.84 percent (size 84) to 8.60 percent (size 40) on average in the VAR model.

Finally, the pandemic affects only avocado shipments of sizes 32, 36, 40, and 48 based on the econometric models. For these respective sizes, avocado shipments are lower by 5.19 percent (size 48) to 8.36 percent (size 36). No statistically significant impacts are evident for avocado shipments of sizes 60, 70, and 84 concerning the pandemic based on the econometric models. The pandemic affects only avocado shipments of sizes 36, 40, 48, and 70 based on the VAR model. For these respective sizes, avocado shipments are lower by 3.68 percent (size 70) to 7.38 percent (size 36). No statistically significant impacts are evident for avocado shipments of sizes 32, 60, and 84 concerning the pandemic based on the VAR model. Thus, the set of models provides different impacts of the pandemic on weekly Hass avocado shipments.

4.1 Weekly Ex-Post Forecasts of Avocado Shipments

We derive ex-post forecasts of weekly avocado shipments by size using the estimated econometric models and the VAR model. That is, the weekly observations from July 3, 2011, to October 24, 2021, serve as the training sample. The weekly observations from October 31, 2021, to January 23, 2022, constitute the out-of-sample period during which all endogenous and predetermined variables are known. This 13-week period then serves as the ex-post forecast time horizon. By comparing the ex-post forecasts with the actual values of avocado shipments by size for this 13-week period, we are in position to measure forecast accuracy/performance based on absolute percent error.

4.1.1 Ex-Post Weekly Forecasts of the Econometric Models: October 31, 2021, to January 23, 2022

The weekly ex-post forecasts of avocado shipments by size for the econometric models in this analysis are exhibited in **Table 2**. The out-of-sample mean absolute percent error (MAPE) by size of avocado shipments over the 13-week period is as follows: (1) 14.16 percent for size 32; (2) 13.09 percent for size 36; (3) 8.65 percent for size 40; (4) 7.63 percent for size 48; (5) 9.09 percent for size 60; (6) 8.47 percent for size 70; and (7) 12.73 percent for size 84. If we sum the avocado shipments by size over the 13-week period, the absolute percent error (APE) is noticeably reduced to: (1) 2.18 percent for size 32; (2) 4.31 percent for size 36; (3) 2.09 percent for size 40; (4) 0.44 percent for size 48; (5) 2.23 percent for size 60; (6) 5.48 percent for size 70; and (7) 10.89 percent for size 84. In addition, we find that the econometric models over forecast shipment sizes of 32, 60, 70, and 84, and under forecast shipment sizes of 36, 40, and 48.

4.1.2 Ex-Post Weekly Forecasts of the VAR Model: October 31, 2021, to January 23, 2022

The weekly ex-post forecasts of avocado shipments by size for the VAR model in this analysis are exhibited in **Table 3**. The out-of-sample mean absolute percent error (MAPE) by size of avocado shipments over the 13-week period is as follows: (1) 17.06 percent for size 32; (2) 11.09 percent for size 36; (3) 10.13 percent for size 40; (4) 6.99 percent for size 48; (5) 8.36 percent for size 60; (6) 13.07 percent for size 70; and (7) 22.27 percent for size 84. If we sum the avocado shipments by size over the 13-week period, we find that the VAR model over forecasts avocado shipments of sizes 32, 60, 70, and 84, and under forecast avocado shipments of sizes 36, 40, and 48. The absolute percent error (APE) associated with the sum of the avocado shipments by size is as follows: (1) 11.80 percent for size 32; (2) 2.67 percent for size 36; (3) 9.70 percent for size 40; (4) 3.05 percent for size 48; (5) 0.99 percent for size 60; (6) 12.09 percent for size 70; and (7) 22.21 percent for size 84.

Based on MAPE, the econometric models provide better out-of-sample forecasting accuracy of avocado shipment sizes of 32, 40, 70, 84. But the VAR model provides

Week Ending	Size 32 Econometric Model Forecasts	Size 32 Econometric Model Actual Values	Size 32 APE %	Size 36 Econometric Model Forecasts	Size 36 Econometric Model Actual Values	Size 36 APE %
10/31/2021	381.60	336.35	13.45	635.60	565.23	12.45
11/07/2021	336.49	382.97	12.14	565.03	761.05	25.76
11/14/2021	334.83	519.00	35.49	558.43	895.00	37.61
11/21/2021	336.49	368.29	8.63	557.15	677.06	17.71
11/28/2021	318.00	367.31	13.42	517.33	545.13	5.10
12/05/2021	329.31	350.39	6.02	550.34	690.14	20.26
12/12/2021	374.24	379.44	1.37	629.69	580.51	8.47
12/19/2021	402.75	349.18	15.34	657.73	632.71	3.95
12/26/2021	345.88	335.48	3.10	547.81	554.58	1.22
01/02/2022	422.79	363.72	16.24	669.44	636.30	5.21
01/09/2022	585.68	480.00	22.02	950.59	805.00	18.09
01/16/2022	574.66	491.75	16.86	902.52	796.81	13.27
01/23/2022	567.92	473.26	20.00	867.31	857.61	1.13
MAPE			14.16			13.09
Total Shipments Over the 13-Week Period	5,310.64	5,197.14	2.18	8,608.97	8,997.13	4.31
Share	1.83	1.83		2.97	3.17	
	Size 40 Econometric Model Forecasts	**Size 40 Econometric Model Actual Values**	**Size 40 APE %**	**Size 48 Econometric Model Forecasts**	**Size 48 Econometric Model Actual Values**	**Size 48 APE %**
10/31/2021	1,450.10	1,318.65	9.97	8,768.08	7,201.39	21.76
11/07/2021	1,333.00	1,534.83	13.15	7,602.40	8,325.94	8.69
11/14/2021	1,351.25	1,983.00	31.86	7,546.83	10,059.00	24.97
11/21/2021	1,373.03	1,469.48	6.56	7,538.97	7,488.08	0.68
11/28/2021	1,281.08	1,350.85	5.16	6,976.40	6,844.98	1.92
12/05/2021	1,315.29	1,318.78	0.26	7,193.09	7,423.32	3.10
12/12/2021	1,460.27	1,501.56	2.75	8,066.19	7,541.12	6.96
12/19/2021	1,528.73	1,530.78	0.13	8,283.57	8,035.67	3.08
12/26/2021	1,239.62	1,353.04	8.38	6,463.23	6,749.94	4.25
01/02/2022	1,444.44	1,412.01	2.30	7,139.76	7,341.54	2.75
01/09/2022	2,057.41	1,789.00	15.00	9,962.37	8,936.00	11.49
01/16/2022	1,987.84	1,834.51	8.36	9,736.56	9,005.40	8.12
01/23/2022	1,937.06	1,784.96	8.52	9,601.86	9,471.32	1.38
MAPE			8.65			7.63
Total Shipments Over the 13-Week Period	19,759.12	20,181.45	2.09	104,879.31	104,423.70	0.44
Share	6.81	7.11		36.13	36.78	

Week Ending	Size 60 Econometric Model Forecasts	Size 60 Econometric Model Actual Values	APE %	Size 70 Econometric Model Forecasts	Size 70 Econometric Model Actual Values	Size 70 APE %
10/31/2021	7,026.11	5,304.07	32.47	4,201.42	3,259.63	28.89
11/07/2021	6,025.71	6,226.88	3.23	3,602.64	3,311.36	8.80
11/14/2021	5,953.48	6,954.00	14.39	3,478.10	3,599.00	3.36
11/21/2021	5,917.22	5,264.35	12.40	3,395.57	2,951.70	15.04
11/28/2021	5,484.31	5,028.20	9.07	3,114.68	2,709.93	14.94
12/05/2021	5,635.94	5,304.49	6.25	3,228.04	3,008.71	7.29
12/12/2021	6,306.59	5,748.60	9.71	3,583.05	3,343.45	7.17
12/19/2021	6,389.35	6,620.06	3.49	3,558.31	3,465.78	2.67
12/26/2021	4,928.56	5,683.14	13.28	2,770.05	3,105.52	10.80
01/02/2022	5,198.11	5,528.54	5.98	2,841.29	2,942.64	3.44
01/09/2022	7,097.62	6,818.00	4.10	3,846.23	3,710.00	3.67
01/16/2022	7,137.48	6,886.07	3.65	3,939.41	3,918.44	0.54
01/23/2022	7,172.62	7,159.17	0.19	4,014.78	3,879.23	3.49
MAPE			9.09			8.47
Total Shipments Over the 13-Week Period	80,273.10	78,525.57	2.23	45,573.57	43,205.39	5.48
Share	27.65	27.66		15.70	15.22	

	Size 84 Econometric Model Forecasts	Size 84 Econometric Model Actual Values	Size 84 APE %
10/31/2021	2,291.82	1,793.39	27.79
11/07/2021	2,057.29	1,672.39	23.01
11/14/2021	2,020.47	1,899.00	6.40
11/21/2021	1,997.70	1,587.21	25.86
11/28/2021	1,858.10	1,537.38	20.86
12/05/2021	1,889.44	1,509.03	25.21
12/12/2021	2,036.63	1,939.23	5.02
12/19/2021	2,039.79	1,852.42	10.11
12/26/2021	1,581.65	1,667.00	5.12
01/02/2022	1,580.41	1,511.98	4.53
01/09/2022	2,120.85	1,962.00	8.10
01/16/2022	2,186.93	2,147.58	1.83
01/23/2022	2,241.58	2,279.70	1.67
MAPE			12.73
Total Shipments Over the 13-Week Period	25,902.66	23,358.31	10.89
Share	8.92	8.23	

Table 2.
Summary of Ex-Post Forecasts from the Econometric Models of Weekly Shipments by Size, October 31, 2021, to January 23, 2022.

Week Ending	Size 32 VAR Model Forecasts	Size 32 VAR Model Actual Values	Size 32 APE %	Size 36 VAR Model Forecasts	Size 36 VAR Model Actual Values	Size 36 APE %
10/31/2021	376.22	336.35	11.85	606.61	565.23	7.32
11/07/2021	363.6	382.97	5.06	575.93	761.05	24.32
11/14/2021	384.92	519.00	25.83	593.17	895.00	33.72
11/21/2021	401.82	368.29	9.10	614.48	677.06	9.24
11/28/2021	384.97	367.31	4.81	577.44	545.13	5.93
12/05/2021	394.46	350.39	12.58	599.61	690.14	13.12
12/12/2021	434.22	379.44	14.44	661.05	580.51	13.87
12/19/2021	453.36	349.18	29.84	678.43	632.71	7.23
12/26/2021	384.5	335.48	14.61	558.19	554.58	0.65
01/02/2022	448.5	363.72	23.31	654.62	636.30	2.88
01/09/2022	612.35	480.00	27.57	930.26	805.00	15.56
01/16/2022	589.94	491.75	19.97	864.9	796.81	8.55
01/23/2022	581.37	473.26	22.84	842.2	857.61	1.80
MAPE			17.06			11.09
Total Shipments Over the 13-Week Period	5,810.23	5,197.14	11.80	8,756.89	8,997.13	2.67
Share	2.00	1.83		3.02	3.17	
	Size 40 VAR Model Forecasts	**Size 40 VAR Model Actual Values**	**Size 40 APE %**	**Size 48 VAR Model Forecasts**	**Size 48 VAR Model Actual Values**	**Size 48 APE %**
10/31/2021	1,351.96	1,318.65	2.53	8,412.14	7,201.39	16.81
11/07/2021	1,279.05	1,534.83	16.67	7,412.38	8,325.94	10.97
11/14/2021	1,300.26	1,983.00	34.43	7,387.08	10,059.00	26.56
11/21/2021	1,324.29	1,469.48	9.88	7,415.18	7,488.08	0.97
11/28/2021	1,233.30	1,350.85	8.70	6,849.73	6,844.98	0.07
12/05/2021	1,244.27	1,318.78	5.65	7,067.63	7,423.32	4.79
12/12/2021	1,362.11	1,501.56	9.29	7,901.41	7,541.12	4.78
12/19/2021	1,418.74	1,530.78	7.32	8,108.15	8,035.67	0.90
12/26/2021	1,133.86	1,353.04	16.20	6,286.76	6,749.94	6.86
01/02/2022	1,298.45	1,412.01	8.04	6,915.74	7,341.54	5.80
01/09/2022	1,841.03	1,789.00	2.91	9,538.17	8,936.00	6.74
01/16/2022	1,741.06	1,834.51	5.09	8,986.52	9,005.40	0.21
01/23/2022	1,696.26	1,784.96	4.97	8,958.66	9,471.32	5.41
MAPE			10.13			6.99
Total Shipments Over the 13-Week Period	18,224.64	20,181.45	9.70	101,239.55	104,423.70	3.05
Share	6.28	7.11		34.87	36.78	

	Size 60 VAR Model Forecasts	Size 60 VAR Model Actual Values	Size 60 APE %	Size 70 VAR Model Forecasts	Size 70 VAR Model Actual Values	Size 70 APE %
10/31/2021	6,640.06	5,304.07	25.19	3,859.67	3,259.63	18.41
11/07/2021	5,804.66	6,226.88	6.78	3,374.57	3,311.36	1.91
11/14/2021	5,804.97	6,954.00	16.52	3,406.20	3,599.00	5.36
11/21/2021	5,795.43	5,264.35	10.09	3,446.34	2,951.70	16.76
11/28/2021	5,431.96	5,028.20	8.03	3,274.24	2,709.93	20.82
12/05/2021	5,648.83	5,304.49	6.49	3,531.62	3,008.71	17.38
12/12/2021	6,343.34	5,748.60	10.35	4,008.05	3,343.45	19.88
12/19/2021	6,478.06	6,620.06	2.14	4,027.62	3,465.78	16.21
12/26/2021	4,967.52	5,683.14	12.59	3,138.62	3,105.52	1.07
01/02/2022	5,238.02	5,528.54	5.25	3,210.35	2,942.64	9.10
01/09/2022	7,084.24	6,818.00	3.90	4,298.21	3,710.00	15.85
01/16/2022	6,942.89	6,886.07	0.83	4,311.87	3,918.44	10.04
01/23/2022	7,120.34	7,159.17	0.54	4,542.62	3,879.23	17.10
MAPE			8.36			13.07
Total Shipments Over the 13-Week Period	79,300.32	78,525.57	0.99	48,429.98	43,205.39	12.09
Share	27.32	27.66		16.68	15.22	

Week Ending	**Size 84 VAR Model Forecasts**	**Size 84 VAR Model Actual Values**	**Size 84 APE %**
	Size 84	**Size 84**	**Size 84**
10/31/2021	2,085.34	1,793.39	16.28
11/07/2021	1,923.59	1,672.39	15.02
11/14/2021	1,936.66	1,899.00	1.98
11/21/2021	1,946.07	1,587.21	22.61
11/28/2021	1,885.98	1,537.38	22.67
12/05/2021	2,074.63	1,509.03	37.48
12/12/2021	2,330.93	1,939.23	20.20
12/19/2021	2,403.42	1,852.42	29.74
12/26/2021	1,895.91	1,667.00	13.73
01/02/2022	1,910.83	1,511.98	26.38
01/09/2022	2,622.32	1,962.00	33.66
01/16/2022	2,680.18	2,147.58	24.80
01/23/2022	2,850.00	2,279.70	25.02
MAPE			22.27
Total Shipments Over the 13-Week Period	28,545.86	23,358.31	22.21
Share	9.83	8.23	

Table 3.
Summary of Ex-Post Forecasts from the Vector Autoregression Models of Weekly Shipments by Size, October 31, 2021, to January 23, 2022.

better out-of-sample forecast accuracy of avocado shipments of sizes 36, 48, and 60. If we sum avocado shipments by size over the 13-week ex-post period, based on APE, the econometric models provide better out-of-sample forecasting accuracy for sizes 32, 40, 48, 70 and 84. The VAR model yields better out-of-sample forecast performance for sizes 36 and 60 if we sum avocado shipments by size over the 13-week ex-post period. Hence, neither the econometric models nor the VAR model provides better forecast accuracy universally across all avocado shipment sizes. As well, as exhibited in **Tables 2** and **3**, the forecasted and actual shares of the respective shipment sizes align very well across the board over the 13-week period from October 31, 2021, to January 23, 2022.

5. Concluding remarks

Both the econometric models and the VAR model allow us to discern the impacts of inflation-adjusted and exchange-rate adjusted prices per box as well as inflation-adjusted and exchange-rate adjusted U.S. disposable income, holidays and events, and seasonality on the level of Hass avocado shipments by size. In general, these impacts are robust across the class of models by shipment size. As well, the respective class of models mimic the variability in the level of shipments by size quite well based on goodness-of-fit metrics. Moreover, based on absolute percent error, the respective class of models provide reasonably accurate forecasts of the level of Hass avocado shipments by size. Going forward, we recommend generating weekly *ex-ante* forecasts on a continual basis based on the econometric models and the VAR model. These respective forecasts would provide lower and upper bounds of the level of Hass avocado shipments from Mexico to the United States by size to stakeholders in the industry.

Acknowledgements

We gratefully acknowledge the Mexican Hass Avocado Importer Association who provided financial support as well as the data for this study.

Conflict of interest

No conflicts of interest exist concerning this study.

Jel classification

JEL Codes: C13, C32, C53.

Author details

Oral Capps
Texas A&M University, College Station, Texas, United States of America

*Address all correspondence to: oral.capps@ag.tamu.edu

References

[1] Samuelson PA. Economic forecasting and science. The Michigan Quarterly Review. 1965:274-280

[2] Healthline. 12 Proven Health Benefits of Avocado [Internet]. 2019. Available from: https://www.healthline.com/nutrition/12-proven-benefits-of-avocado. [Accessed: May 24, 2022]

[3] Shahbandeh M. Statista. Per capita consumption of fresh avocados in the United States from 2000 to 2020 [Internet]. 2021. Available from: https://www.statista.com/statistics/257192/per-capita-consumption-of-fresh-avocados-in-the-us/. [Accessed: May 24, 2022]

[4] Agricultural Marketing Resource Center. Avocados [Internet]. 2022. Available from: https://www.agmrc.org/commodities-products/fruits/avocados/. [Accessed: May 24, 2022]

[5] Peterson EB, Orden D. Avocado pests and avocado trade. American Journal of Agricultural Economics. 2008;**90**: 321-335

[6] Shahbandeh M. Statista. Global avocado production in 2020, by country [Internet]. 2022. Available from: https://www.statista.com/statistics/593211/global-avocado-production-by-country/. [Accessed: May 24, 2022]

[7] Theil H. Applied economic forecasting. North-Holland Publishing Company; 1966

[8] Clements MP, Hendry DF. A companion to economic forecasting. First ed. Blackwell Publishing; 2002

[9] Diebold FX. Elements of forecasting. 4th ed. South-Western Cengage Learning; 2008

[10] Sims CA. Macroeconomics and reality. Econometrica. 1980;**48**(1):1-48

[11] Mexican Hass Avocado Importer Association (MHAIA) [Internet]. Available from: https://mhaia.org/. [Accessed: May 1, 2022]

[12] Hass Avocado Board [Internet]. Available from: https://www.hassavocadoboard.com. [Accessed: May 01, 2022]

[13] Zellner A. An efficient method of estimating seemingly unrelated regressions and tests for aggregation bias. Journal of the American Statistical Association. Jun 1962;**57**(298):348-367

[14] Belsley DA, Kuh K, Welsch RE. Regression diagnostics: Identifying influential data and sources of collinearity. New York: John Wiley and Sons; 1980

Chapter 4

Spatiotemporal Difference-in-Differences: A Dynamic Mechanism of Socio-Economic Evaluation

Lijia Mo

Abstract

Advances in econometric modeling and analysis of spatial cross-sectional and spatial panel data assist in revealing the spatiotemporal characteristics behind socio-economic phenomena and improving prediction accuracy. Difference-in-differences (DID) is frequently used in causality inference and estimation of the treatment effect of the policy intervention in different time and space dimensions. Relying on flexible distributional hypotheses of treatment versus experiment groups on spillover, spatiotemporal DID provides space for innovation and alternatives, given the spatial heterogeneity, dependence, and proximity into consideration. This chapter gives a practical econometric evaluation of the dynamic mechanism in this spatiotemporal context as well as a toolkit for this fulfillment.

Keywords: spatial difference-in-differences (SDID), causality inference, spillover, random effects, fixed effects, direct effects

1. Introduction

Spatial panel data are used to investigate the spatial reliance in different regions, and some of the spillover effects are between regions, and ordinary least squares cannot reveal.

Spatial difference-in-differences (SDID) is used to investigate policy effect on the socio-economic variable, given the temporal-lagged variable into consideration. Usually, OLS fails to estimate the model with unbiased that Moran's I reveals. The function of segregation of direct, indirect, and total effects in terms of the specification of the fixed and random effect model makes the SDID's advantage over the traditional DID model.

2. Assumptions of SDID

2.1 DID model assumptions

To study the fixed effect of individual and time respectively, difference-in-differences (DID) specify the time and location designs in an experiment setting by an estimator of the fixed effect of panel data in average treatment effect on the treated [1, 2]. However, the spatial spillover effect complicates the estimation process. In the experiment group and treatment group, the impact of the treatment is measured before and after the treatment is applied.

Spatial Policy Effect:

$$Y_{it} = \mu_t + C_i + \tau D_{it} + \varepsilon_{it} \tag{1}$$

Individual fixed effect C_i captures the difference between the treatment and control groups on the time-invariant characteristic. μ_t, the temporal fixed effect of time-variant characteristics between control and treatment groups, is assumed to be of the same variance between the control and treatment groups on time-variant characteristics with respect to a specific time.

Time-variant control D_{it} satisfies conditional independence assumption (CIA) to work as a core in the causality inference, while assuming time is exogenous, that is, $E[\varepsilon_{it}|treatment, time] = 0$.

The ordinary least square (OLS) is a consistent estimator for the effect of the causality inference.

$$\tau = E[Y_{i1}(1) - Y_{i1}(0)|D_i = 1] \tag{2}$$

After the bias is removed, $E[\hat{\tau}] = \tau + Treatment\ group\ Spillover + Control\ group\ Spillover + Spillover\ between\ different\ group\ type$

So far, only the spillover between treatment and control groups is not treated.

$$D_{it} = \left(D_{it}^{(1)} - \overline{D}^{(1)}\right) \times \left(D_{it}^{(2)} - \overline{D}^{(2)}\right) \tag{3}$$

D_{it} is DID, the interaction term of temporal and spatial difference; that is, $\hat{\beta}_{DID}$ in **Figure 1**, the observable time-dependent variable as control. $D_{it}^{(1)}$ is a dummy variable to denote the group being treated, valued at 1; or group not being treated, values at 0. $D_{it}^{(2)}$ is a dummy variable indicating a local policy or temporal element, values at 1 in

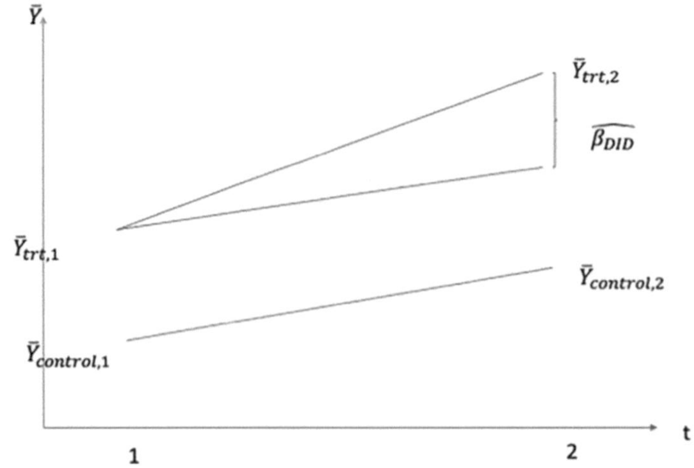

Figure 1.
DID estimation illustration.

the year of policy implementation and thereafter, or 0 for the years before. $\overline{D}^{(1)}\overline{D}^{(2)}$ are the means of two dummy variables.

The strict set of assumptions of the DID is there is no spillover in treatment, control, or between treatment and control groups. When an assumption of same spillover effect within the control and treatment groups is added to the strict set, the assumption becomes relaxed restriction set 1. When there is no spillover between treatment and control groups, the assumption of relaxed restriction set 1 is changed to the spillover effect on control and treatment groups are same and the assumption becomes relaxed restriction set 2.

$$\hat{\tau} = \hat{E}[Y_{i1} - Y_{i0}|D_i = 1] - \hat{E}[Y_{i1} - Y_{i0}|D_i = 0] \tag{4}$$

$\hat{E}[Y_{i1} - Y_{i0}|D_i = 1]$: Counterfactual trend + τ +treatment group spatial spillover
$\hat{E}[Y_{i1} - Y_{i0}|D_i = 0]$: Counterfactual trend + control group spatial spillover
The traditional DID

$$\tau = E[Y_{i1}(1) - Y_{i1}(0)|D_i = 1] \tag{5}$$

2.2 Spatial model assumptions

The spatial spillover has the properties of spatial heterogeneity, spatial dependence (the butterfly effect and spatial association), and spatial proximity. Spatial heterogeneity denotes the different structures of spatial units in different locations [3–5]. Without the assumption on spatial homogeneity parameters, it is hard to estimate the model with the increase of observations. In the spatial model, most of the estimation assumes locations are regional homogeneous. The definition of spatial heterogeneity is the non-smoothness of a spatial random process, which comprises change of function form or parameters and heteroscedasticity of two categories.

Spatial dependence means the adjacent spatial locations have the propensity to be associated with each other and work in coordination synchronously.

Spatial proximity denotes that in spatial areas everything is related to everything else, but near things are more related than distant things (Waldo Tobler).

3. Model specifications-generalized spatial model

The panel data regression is a linear regression with the combination of three types of spatially lagged variables across time, which traces the same observation unit over different times. The observation unit's characteristic over time and spatial location are the research interest. The classical panel data regression takes the following form based on Arbia [6], Cerulli [2], LeSage and Pace [3], and Wooldridge [5]:

$$y_{it} = X_{it}\beta + c_i + v_{it} \tag{6}$$

$i = 1,2, \ldots N$ index corresponding to i^{th} different observation units in the cross-sectional data.

$t = 1,2, \ldots T$ denotes time. c_i is fixed effect w.r.t. observation unit, or spatial specific effect invariant to time. Alternatively, or simultaneously, c_t a time-specific fixed effect w.r.t. different time, and invariant to observation unit can be embedded to the model. v_{it} is an independent identical distributed error term, iid. $(0, \sigma^2)$.

The generalized spatial model includes the following variations.
Spatial Autoregression Model (SAR-SDID)

$$y_{it} = \rho \sum_{j=1}^{N} \omega_{ij} y_{jt} + X_{it}\beta + \tau D() + c_i + v_{it} \tag{7}$$

Before the spatial regression, Moran's I test is used to measure and test spatial autoregression in general. It is also called a global spatial autoregression test; that is, it measures the degree of similarity to each other between the spatial observations in the sample.

$$I = \frac{n}{\sum_i \sum_j \omega_{ij}} \frac{\sum_i \sum_j \omega_{ij} (x_i - \overline{x})(x_j - \overline{x})}{\sum_i (x_i - \overline{x})^2} \tag{8}$$

where n is the number of observations, and ω_{ij} is the element in i^{th} row and j^{th} column from the spatial weight matrix W. x_i, x_j are i^{th} and j^{th} observation in the spatial unit, and $\overline{x}$ is the average of the observations.

The positive Moran's I denotes a positive correlation, while a negative value means a negative correlation. The standardization of the spatial weight matrix simplifies the notation as follows.

$$I = \frac{X'WX}{X'X} \tag{9}$$

It is obvious that Moran's I is the Pearson correlation coefficient between X and WX. It follows an asymptotic distribution, which simplifies the process of using Moran's I to test spatial autocorrelation in the residual of the test. It is a statistical inference through the z-test.

A partial Moran's test is

$$I_i = \frac{n(x_i - \overline{x}) \sum_{i \neq j} \omega_{ij} (x_j - \overline{x})}{\sum_i (x_i - \overline{x})^2} \tag{10}$$

Partial Moran's test I_i averages over i is the overall Moran's I. Partial Moran's test I_i is often used. Overall Moran's I is the slope of the scatter plot as in **Figure 2**, where the X-axis denotes X and Y-axis denotes lagged variable WX of X. The slope of the line reflects the relation between the observed variable and the spatial lagged observed variable. The line across the 1st and 3rd coordinates denotes a positive spatial correlation.

'Columbus' data are generated by geographical information systems (GIS) [7] based on US census data[1] on Columbus boundary systems, with the data type ".shp." The file stores feature geometry such as coordinates of polygon centroids and their boundary. The W matrix is derived from the contiguity-based neighbors' list [6].

The summary statistics of the "crime" variable in the "Columbus" data, totally 49 observations, are as follows (**Table 1**):

[1] http://www.census.gov/geo/maps-data/data/tiger-line.html

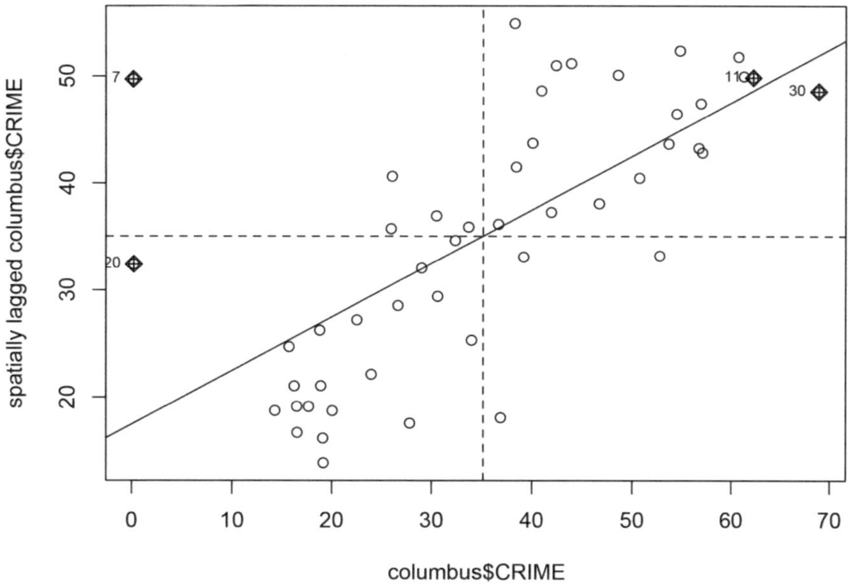

Figure 2.
Moran's I scatter plot of Columbus crime data.

Minimum	1st quantile	Median	Mean	3rd quantile	Maximum
0.1783	20.0485	34.0008	35.1288	48.5855	68.8920

Table 1.
Summary statistics of crime variable.

The test of Moran's I depends on the distribution of its input variable and is done *via* Monte Carlo simulation. Through the random multiple interchanging location of the spatial units, the model recalculates the weight matrix W and Moran's I statistic to obtain Moran's I after multiple replacements. In a frequency rectangle picture, Moran's I empirical distribution is developed and compared with the statistic from the direct calculation.

The assumption of the method is when the spatial units are randomly distributed, the variable is not autocorrelated, and Moran's I is close to 0. When Moran's I is with a low probability of occurrence, the null hypothesis of no autocorrelation is rejected. When the input variable is the residual of classical linear regression, assumed to follow a normal distribution, Moran's I follows a normal distribution as well, where the z-test is applicable to avoid the heavy calculation of Monte Carlo simulation.

3.1 Spatial error model (SEM-SDID)

$$y_{it} = X_{it}\beta + \tau D() + c_i + u_{it} \tag{11}$$

$$u_{it} = \rho \sum_{j=1}^{N} m_{ij} u_{jt} + v_{it} \tag{12}$$

3.2 Spatial Durbin model (SDM-SDID)

$$y_{it} = \rho \sum_{j=1}^{N} \omega_{ij} y_{jt} + X_{it}\beta + \sum_{j=1}^{N} \omega_{ij} X_{jt}\theta + \tau D() + \sum_{j=1}^{N} \omega_{ij} D(.) + \pi + c_i + v_{it} \tag{13}$$

3.3 Spatial lag of X model (SXL-SDID)

$$y_{it} = X_{it}\beta + \sum_{j=1}^{N} \omega_{ij} X_{jt}\theta + \tau D() + c_i + \sum_{j=1}^{N} \omega_{ij} D(.) u_{jt} + v_{it} \tag{14}$$

The spatial weight matrix ω_{ij} and m_{ij} are invariant to time changes. Spatial and temporal-specific effects can be treated as fixed or random effects. If treated as a fixed effect, the specific effect is taken as a parameter to estimate. Whereas a random effect, it is treated as a random variable following iid. $(0, \sigma^2)$. The deterministic factor is to tell whether c_i is correlated with X_{it}. The fixed effect is used to treat the correlation, while the random effect is for the uncorrelation. The random effect has the advantage of improving effectiveness with the observation number and distinguishes the factor invariant to time. Because c_i is invariant to time, it is hard to separate observed information from individual effect. ρ the spatial lag term is used to test the spatial spillover effects between neighboring regions [3]. The positively significant coefficient of ρ indicates a positive spatial spillover effect.

To account for the direct impact and indirect impact, the transformation of Eq. 13 is taken as follows.

In matrix format, let the constant vector $\mathbb{1}_n$ and relevant parameters α to be embedded in Eq. 13.

$$y = (I_n - \rho W)^{-1} \mathbb{1}_n \alpha + (I_n - \rho W)^{-1} X\beta + (I_n - \rho W)^{-1} \varepsilon \tag{15}$$

$$y = \sum_{r=1}^{k} S_r(W) X_r + (I_n - \rho W)^{-1} \mathbb{1}_n \alpha + (I_n - \rho W)^{-1} \varepsilon \tag{16}$$

The sum of the rows of $S_r(W)$ denotes the total impact of a region to an observation (ATITO); the sum of columns of $S_r(W)$ is the total impact of a region from an observation (ATIFO). The average of the sum of rows or columns is the average total impact (ATI). The average of elements on the main diagonal is the average direct impact (ADI), and average indirect impact (AII) is defined as the difference between average total impact (ATI) and average direct impact (ADI).

$$S_r(W) = (I_n - \rho W)^{-1} \beta_r = \frac{\partial E(y)}{\partial x_r} = \begin{bmatrix} & \frac{\partial E(y_1)}{\partial x_{1r}} \cdots . & \frac{\partial E(y_1)}{\partial x_{nr}} & \\ \cdots & & & \cdots \\ & \frac{\partial E(y_n)}{\partial x_{1r}} \cdots .. & \frac{\partial E(y_n)}{\partial x_{nr}} & \end{bmatrix} \tag{17}$$

where ADI denotes the average impact of change of local explanatory variable x_r on the specific local dependent variable y.

$$ADI = n^{-1} \sum_{i=1}^{n} \frac{\partial E(y_i)}{\partial x_{ir}} = n^{-1} tr[S_r(W)] \tag{18}$$

ATITO is the average impact on the specific local dependent variable y from the change in the explanatory variable x_r of all regions.

$$ATITO = n^{-1}\sum_{i=1}^{n}\sum_{j=1}^{n} S_r(W)_{ij} = n^{-1}\sum_{i=1}^{n}\sum_{j=1}^{n}\frac{\partial E(y_i)}{\partial x_{jr}} \tag{19}$$

ATIFO is the average impact on all regional dependent variable y from the change in the explanatory variable x_r of a specific region.

$$ATIFO = n^{-1}\sum_{j=1}^{n}\sum_{i=1}^{n} S_r(W)_{ij} = n^{-1}\sum_{j=1}^{n}\sum_{i=1}^{n}\frac{\partial E(y_i)}{\partial x_{jr}} \tag{20}$$

ATITO and ATIFO are equal values and are called by a joint name ATI.

$$\text{AII} = \text{ATI} - \text{ADI} \tag{21}$$

4. Tests on model assumptions

A robust test is performed to study whether the estimation is sensitive to the change in the width of the event window. Wald test follows an asymptotic chi-squared distribution with N degree of freedom.

The test on correlation coefficient ρ is positive significance.

The estimation is done with spatial inverse-distance contiguity weight matrix.

A parallel test is used to test that the change of temporally dependent variable as control will or will not impact the direction of policy influence. A good control ensures the conditional independent assumption (CIA) holds. The different outcomes between the treatment group subject to intervention and the control group in the absence of intervention produce reliable results if both groups are similar in their characteristics and have parallel trends before the intervention, that is, the parallel trends assumption. If the assumption holds, the different outcomes between groups attributed to the intervention ([1, 8–11]). It differs from the Granger test in that a parallel test is performed in the periods before policy intervention to reveal the significant parameters $H0 : \tau_0 = \tau_{-1} = \ldots = \tau_{-k} = 0$ that spans over more than two time periods, while the Granger test requires only a minimum of two periods and is much simpler [12]. If the assumption μ_t of the same fixed time effect of both groups is the same holds, incorporating new control variable X_{it} will not change the estimation of parameters except their variance.

$$Y_{it} = \mu_t + C_i + \tau D_{it} + \varepsilon_{it} \tag{22}$$

$$Y_{it} = \mu_t + C_i + \tau D_{it} + \sum_{k=0}^{m}\tau_{-k}D_{i,t-k} + \sum_{k=1}^{q}\tau_{+k}D_{i,t+k} + X_{it}\beta + \varepsilon_{it} \tag{23}$$

Granger test is focused on the after-event periods, to investigate whether the parameters of DID after the policy intervention, $\tau_1 \ldots \tau_k$, are significant. Using lags and leads provides a test to determine whether past treatments affect the current outcome or for the presence of anticipatory effects, that is, to estimate τ_{-k} and τ_k, thus challenging the conventional idea that causality works only “from the past to the present” [13].

To be specific, Buerger et al. [12] use Granger equations to test the parallel trends assumption, the most important DID framework assumption to improve evidence on causal claims.

	NGP		CAP	
	Model 1	**Model 2**	**Model 3**	**Model 4**
	Fixed effects	**Random effects**	**Fixed effects**	**Random effects**
PGDP	82.174*** (5.91)	77.775*** (5.93)	0.048* (1.65)	0.049** (2.31)
NCU	200.218*** (8.46)	82.571*** (5.16)	0.195*** (3.92)	0.018 (1.17)
TSR	109274.4*** (3.53)	72722.79** (2.55)	230.979*** (3.61)	18.035 (0.38)
NIE	−79.33*** (−2.74)	−52.884* (−1.83)	−0.135** (−2.24)	−0.091** (−2.2)
DID	1592.831** (2.28)	1788.006** (2.48)	4.394*** (3.02)	3.251** (2.24)
Year 2011	−961.286*** (−2.85)	−621.956* (−1.75)	−2.409*** (−3.19)	0.692 (0.88)
… .. Table	Omitted	intentionally		
ρ	0.652*** (7.89)	0.616*** (−7.2)	0.419** (2.58)	1.864* (1.77)
… .. Table	Omitted	intentionally		
Wald test of spatial terms	62.25***	52.83***	6.66**	100.93*

is significant at 0.1.is significant at 0.05.***is significant at 0.001.*

Table 2.
Results of estimation [16].

	NGP		CAP	
	Model 1	**Model 2**	**Model 3**	**Model 4**
	Fixed effects	**Random effects**	**Fixed effects**	**Random effects**
Direct effect	1662.371** (2.28)	1851.767** (2.48)	4.444*** (3.02)	3.392** (2.36)
Indirect effect	2719.377* (1.78)	2617.57* (1.88)	2.914 (1.38)	1.305 (1.13)
Total effect	4381.748** (2.04)	4469.337** (2.21)	7.358** (2.4)	4.697** (2.11)

is significant at 0.1.is significant at 0.05.***is significant at 0.001.*

Table 3.
Results of policy effect tests [16].

The placebo tests in **Table 4** show that there is no change of significance in the DID if the policy is implemented in the year before or after the actual year of implementation. The result is problematic to convince that the incentive patent policy promotes the outcome or commercialization of a patent. The DID is rather a placebo without an effect on the patent on its own, whereas a proxy of province systemic difference makes the diversity.

	NGP		CAP	
	Model 5	**Model 6**	**Model 7**	**Model 8**
	1 year earlier	**1 year later**	**1 year earlier**	**1 year later**
PGDP	82.595*** (5.92)	82.703*** (5.96)	0.049* (1.68)	0.049* (1.7)
NCU	201.749*** (8.5)	199.52*** (8.44)	0.199*** (3.98)	0.195*** (3.91)
TSR	106525.2*** (3.43)	109694.8*** (3.55)	223.24*** (3.48)	230.945*** (3.6)
NIE	−81.847*** (−2.82)	−76.23*** (−2.63)	−0.141** (−2.33)	−0.131** (−2.15)
DID	1480.638* (1.82)	1624.062** (2.5)	4.687*** (2.77)	3.724*** (2.74)
Year 2011	−1040.216*** (−3.06)	−926.287*** (−2.75)	−2.669*** (−3.49)	−2.31*** (−3.06)
Table	Omitted	intentionally		
ρ	0.654*** (7.91)	0.65*** (−7.86)	0.41** (2.5)	0.432*** (2.71)
Table	Omitted	intentionally		
Wald test of spatial terms	62.63***	61.76***	6.23**	7.33*

is significant at 0.1.is significant at 0.05.***is significant at 0.001.*

Table 4.
Results of placebo tests [16].

6. Conclusion

This chapter outlines the methodology and application of DID in spatial analysis. The impact of incentive policy on economic activities is controversial. The empirical evidence results from a correlation test rather than causality analysis. SDID as a tool to segregate the direct effect, indirect effect, and total effect in the fixed-effect and random-effect models finds a causal relationship between the policy and relevant economic activities under the influence while dealing with the spillover effects in quasi-natural experiments. The placebo effect of policy can expand the horizon of policy evaluation, which helps consolidate the scientific foundation of policy evaluation. Regional policies are proxies for other variables that characterize the systemic differences in policies between regions.

In the policy evaluation, the SDID reveals the spatial spillover effect on the neighborhood regions, causing them to imitate the policies and promote economic activities. It is not appropriate to study the policy effect independently, but a comprehensive evaluation from a local perspective is preferred.

Acknowledgements

I thank Jiafeng Gu, Tongying Liang, and Feifei Liang for their generous comments.

Conflict of interest

The author declare no conflict of interest.

A. Appendix

Stata Code

```
/*Create time fixed effect and individual fixed effects.*/
sort time id
by time: gen ind = _n
sort id time
by id: gen T = _n
/*Generate treat and post two dummy variables, with 2010 set as time spot of policy intervention and observations from 17 to 31 are treatment group, and rest is control group.*/
gen treat = 0
replace treat = 1 if id >17
gen after = 0
replace after = 1 if time > = 2010
/* Create Weight matrix:*/
spmatrix create idistance M /*spatial inversed distance matrix*/
spmatrix dir
spmatrix create contiguity W/*spatial distance matrix*/
spmatrix dir

estat moran, errorlag (W)
estat moran, errorlag (M)

gen treatafter = treat*after
spmatrix create contiguity W if year == 2010
spxtregress NGP treatafter PGDP NCU TSR NIE i.time,re dvarlag (W)

gen treatafter = treat*after
spmatrix create contiguity W if year == 2010
spxtregress CAP treatafter PGDP NCU TSR NIE i.time,re dvarlag (W)
/*General application*/
1)SAR-SDID
> spmatrix create contiguity W if year == 2010
>spxtregress NGP treatafter PGDP NCU TSR NIE i.time, re dvarlag (W)

2)SEM-SDID
> spmatrix create contiguity W if year == 2010
>spxtregress NGP treatafter PGDP NCU TSR NIE i.time,re errorlag (W)

3)SDM-SDID
> spmatrix create contiguity W if year == 2010
>spxtregress NGP treatafter PGDP NCU TSR NIE i.time, re dvarlag (W) ivarlag (W: X)
```

4)SXL-SDID

```
> spmatrix create contiguity W if year == 2010
>spxtregress NGP treatafter PGDP NCU TSR NIE i.time,re ivarlag (W: DX)
```

Author details

Lijia Mo
Suzhou University, Suzhou, Anhui, China

*Address all correspondence to: molijia@hotmail.com

References

[1] Angrist JD, Pischke J. Mostly Harmless Econometrics: An Empiricist's Companion. Princeton, NJ: Princeton University Press; 2008

[2] Cerulli G. Econometric Evaluation of Socio-Economic Programs: Theory and Applications. Advanced Studies in Theoretical and Applied Econometrics. Vol. 49. Heidelberg: Springer; 2015

[3] LeSage JL, Pace RK. Introduction to Spatial Econometrics. London, UK: Boca Raton: Chapman and Hall/CRC press; 2009

[4] Wooldridge JM. Econometric Analysis of Cross Section and Panel Data. Cambridge, MA: MIT Press; 2010

[5] Wooldridge JM. Introductory Econometrics: A Modern Approach. Boston, MA: Cengage Learning; 2015

[6] Arbia G. A Primer for Spatial Econometrics: With Applications in R. Basingstoke: Palgrave Macmillan; 2014

[7] Burrough PA, Mcdonnell RA, Lloyd CD. Principles of Geographical Information Systems. 3rd ed. Oxford: Oxford; 2014

[8] Angrist JD, Pischke J. Mastering Metrics: The Path from Cause to Effect. Princeton, NJ: Princeton University Press; 2015

[9] Meyer BD. Natural and quasi-experiments in economics. Journal of Business and Statistics. 1995;**13**(2): 151-161

[10] Pomeranz D. Impact evaluation methods in public economics: A brief introduction to randomized evaluations and comparison with other methods. Public Finance Review. 2017;**45**(1):10-43

[11] St Clair T, Cook TD. Difference-in-differences methods in public finance. National Tax Journal. 2015;**68**(2): 319-338

[12] Buerger C, Sandel RM, Reitano V, Lofton ML, Jones P. Extending differences-in-differences frameworks to Granger equations: Evidence from cutback management during three recessions. International Journal of Public Sector Management. 2021;**34**(6): 688-705

[13] Granger CWJ. Investigating causal relations by econometric models and cross-spectral methods. Econometrica. 1969;**37**(3):424-438

[14] Carlson DE, Cowen JM, Fleming DJ. Third-party governance and performance measurement: A case study of publicly funded private school vouchers. Journal of Public Administration Research and Theory. 2014;**24**(4):897-922

[15] Athey S, Imbens GW. The state of applied econometrics: Causality and policy evaluation. Journal of Economic Perspective. 2017;**31**(2):3-32

[16] Gu J. Effects of patent policy on outputs and commercialization of academic patents in China: A spatial difference-in-differences analysis. Sustainability. 2021;**13**:13459

Chapter 5

The Impact of Inflation Expectations and Public Debt on Taxation in South Africa

Thobeka Ncanywa and Noko Setati

Abstract

The study investigates the impact of inflation expectations and public debt on taxation in South Africa, employing the autoregressive distributive lag model and Granger Causality techniques. The results indicate a long-run positive significant relationship between inflation expectations and taxation and a negative significant relationship between public debt and taxation. This reveals that when consumers and businesses expect the inflation rate to rise, taxable income will also increase. The public debt-taxation nexus can imply that the South African government finances its debts through borrowing than through taxation. Therefore, economic participants must have full knowledge of what can influence taxation.

Keywords: taxation, inflation expectations, public debt, ARDL approach, granger causality

1. Introduction

In South African economic history, the maintenance of price stability and debt stability has always been the major macroeconomic objective that South African policymakers must strive to achieve. In the world of globalization, the cross-border transmission of inflationary forces is undeniable and one of the dynamic macroeconomic issues confronting most economies around the world [1]. Therefore, the risks of inflation must be managed prudently and with caution. South Africa's public debt has always remained a challenge for policymakers. For example, [2] states that policymakers still do not grasp what drives inflation expectations almost 10 years after the Great Recession of 2008–2009. In February 2000, the South African Reserve Bank (SARB) adopted the inflation target as a guideline, which describes an acceptable inflation rate in South Africa. However, inflation risks should be quantified into inflation expectations, and policymakers must consider them. Tax authorities when formulating tax systems, because if tax rates are not adjusted for inflation, this may lead to distortions in the economy [3]. Therefore, the primary aim of this research study is to give attention to how public debt and inflation expectations influence taxation.

Economic participants such as investors, financial analysts, workers, trade unions, and businesses all have opinions on the future rate of inflation, which are referred to as inflation expectations or expected inflation. As a result, people evaluate this rate when making judgments about various economic activities that they want to engage in shortly. In the world of central banking, inflation expectations serve at least two purposes. They provide a summary of statistics where inflation is expected to be because they are essential inputs into the price level. Secondly, they can be used to judge the central bank's inflation target's legitimacy. According to [4], the expected inflation for 2021 was estimated to be 4.6% in 2020 and 5.1% in 2021. Inflation expectations reversed course in the second quarter of the 2021–2022 financial year after declining by 0.3 percentage points relative to the fourth quarter in the previous survey, and on average inflation is expected to edge up from 4.2% in 2021 to 4.4% in 2022 and 4.5% in 2023 [5]. The trend analysis for the two conductors of the inflation expectations surveys depicts a stable price level in South Africa. Hence, on average inflation is expected to be within the official inflation target (3–6%). The rate of inflation expectation affects the behavior of various economic participants on how they should spend and invest, thus affecting taxable income [6].

The study on the effect of inflation expectations and public debt on taxation is important in South Africa. Researchers in South Africa have attempted to establish the link between public debt and taxation. For example, a study by [7] attempted to study the relationship between public debt, economic growth, and inflation based on data among BRICS countries. Based on the literature reviewed in this study, most studies around the world only focused on the relationship between inflation and public debt, which are the explanatory variables in this study [8–10]. From the literature review, it appears that there is a lack of studies about the effects of inflation expectations and public debt on taxation in South Africa. The studies reviewed do not link inflation expectation to public debt and taxation. Therefore, this study will make a significant contribution to the existing body of knowledge in South Africa, because of the unique selection of variables in the specified model. The study adopts the Autoregressive Distributive Lag (ARDL) estimation method for empirical analysis covering the period from 2000 to 2020, which includes the global financial crisis and two health crises.

As alluded to above, non-inflation-adjusted tax rates create distortions in the economy. However, taxation is also a distortion because there is no economic activity involved. Such small negligence in policy decision-making can be problematic, for example, by overestimating or underestimating the true value of the economic activity. Tax thresholds often do not increase in line with inflation [11]. If employees gain a salary increase to match inflation, then they are not better off in real terms. In addition, with a nominal salary increase, individuals may enter a higher tax bracket and therefore be worse off. This phenomenon is called bracket creep. In South Africa, a progressive personal income tax system is used to reduce inequality [12].

2. Literature review

This section is divided into two subsections, which are theoretical literature and empirical literature. The first subsection outlines theories associated with economic time series variables understudy. The second subsection presents empirical evidence related to the topic under review.

2.1 Theoretical literature

The study investigates the influence of inflation expectations and public debt on taxation, which may create distortions in the economy. The fiscal theory of the price level is proposed as a suitable theory that attempts to form and explain the nature of the relationship between inflation expectations and taxation in this study. This theory originates from the work of Woodford in 1994 [13]. This theory emphasizes the role of fiscal policy, including taxes (present and future taxes) and the debt level in determining inflation [14]. Traditionally, this role is tasked to the monetary policy as advocated in the Quantity Theory of money by Friedman in 1980. This theory opposes the monetarist view that states that the money supply is the primary determinant of the price level and inflation [13]. However, both theories share a common view on how an increase in government spending (through public debt) represents an injection in the economy and this increases the flow of money In the end, price levels are expected to increase because of the notion that too much money ceases few goods (ceteris paribus).

The fiscal theory of the price level suggests that in real terms, the government can inflate its debt away [14]. This means that high inflationary pressures caused by the fiscal policy will devalue government debt and the amount that must be repaid will be smaller in real terms. In terms of this theory, high price levels do not warrant the need for present and future tax increases. However, understanding that tax cuts and increases in government spending do not necessarily have to be paid by higher taxes later, may create room for too much government and unstable government debt. This theory will be tested against the Ricardian equivalence hypothesis, which will be reviewed in this subsection.

Ricardian equivalence hypothesis is proposed in this study, because of how it differs from the fiscal theory of the price level on taxation perspective when government increases spending. Ricardo in 1951 developed this theory, which was later elaborated upon by Barro in 1979 [15]. This theory assumes that economic participants are rational, and this allows them to anticipate an increase in taxes when government increases spending. According to this theory, all government purchases must be paid by taxes. Unlike the fiscal theory of the price level, this theory does not consider inflation expectations caused by an increase in government spending through borrowing [16]. Government debt must be repaid by increasing taxes. This theory for the interest of this study anticipates an increase in taxes when public debt increases. This theory suggests that a tax cut today is balanced by tax increases in the future.

This economic theory suggests that when a government tries to stimulate growth in the economy by increasing debt-financed government spending will lead to a tax increase in the future [14]. Therefore, an increase in debt-financed government spending has a positive relationship in the long run. Public debt and taxation are important instruments of fiscal policy [16]. This theory demonstrates the relationship between the two instruments in the economy. In addition, this theory advocates that those taxpayers should anticipate that they will have to pay higher taxes later.

2.2 Empirical literature

Some views in the literature indicate the effects of public debt on expected inflation. For instance, there is a study that investigated fiscal policy and expected inflation in households in the United States [17]. The study used a large-scale survey of US households to assess whether expected inflation reacts to the information provided.

The study employed a Nielsen home scan panel, which included approximately 80,000 households to run the results. The findings revealed that most households do not perceive current high deficits or current debts as inflationary or as the indicator of significant changes in the fiscal outlook [17].

Although a considerable amount of research has been conducted on the issues of public debt and expected inflation, there is a research gap on the impact of inflation expectations and public debt on taxation especially in South Africa [17–19]. For instance, there is a South African study that employed the Autoregressive Distributive Lag (ARDL) to evaluate the nexus between inflation expectations and aggregated demand using secondary time series data [18]. The study revealed that when employing the Error Correction Model (ECM), a 1% increase in inflation expectations would lead to a 0.4% decrease in the level of gross domestic product, ceteris paribus. Since a shadow economy cannot be taxed, it destroys the tax base and reduces the tax revenues, forcing governments to resort to other ways to finance their expenditure [18]. In supporting this statement, another study measured the impact of the shadow economy on inflation and taxation using panel data of 162 countries from 1999 to 2007 [19]. The study observed that there is a positive relationship between the size of the shadow economy and inflation and that the size of the shadow economy and the tax burden are negatively related. From both relations, there have been causal effects running from the shadow economy and tax burden. The relationships are robust in controlling the debt ratio, estimating the two relations as a system, and using alternative estimates of the shadow economy [19].

Some researchers found contradictions in the relationship between taxation, public debt, and the inflation rate using different methodologies. For example, one researcher used an ordinary least square (OLS) methodology to find the negative effects of taxation on macroeconomic aggregates, including inflation in Nigeria [20]. Others used autoregressive distributed lag (ARDL) and discovered that the impact of public debt on inflation is positive but statistically insignificant [9, 21, 22]. The positive association is in line with the study that investigated public debt and inflation nexus using a panel of 52 African countries [7]. Contrary to the findings, it was discovered that a negative relationship exists between the inflation rate and public debt [23].

There was an examination of public debt, budget deficit, and tax policy reforms for fiscal consolidation in Sri Lanka that employed the Vector Error Correction model (VECM) [10]. It was revealed that direct government tax revenue, indirect tax revenue, and consumer price index are negatively correlated with government debt to GDP ratio in the long run. In the short run, only direct tax revenue affects it significantly [10]. In addition, there was an examination of the effects of tax policy on inflation in Nigeria, employing Johansen cointegration test technique [24]. The results of the estimates revealed that the personal income tax rate harms inflation in the long run, while the company income tax rate has a significant positive relationship with inflation in the long run. However, some researchers found conflicting results that personal income tax and company income tax have no significant relationship with GDP [25].

Many scholars utilized Granger Causality tests to reveal the direction of causality in the relations between taxation, public debt, and expected inflation [10, 26–30]. It was revealed that a unidirectional causality relationship exists between tax revenue and public debt [10, 26]. However, few studies revealed that there is a unidirectional causality running from inflation to taxation [27, 28]. Others established a unidirectional relationship between inflation to domestic debt and external debt in Malaysia [29]. In Bangladesh, the results of a study indicated the presence of unidirectional causality running from budget deficit to inflation [30]. This budget deficit is a representation of public borrowing requirements.

In South Africa, a study investigated the relationship between oil prices, exchange rates, and inflation expectations in South Africa [31]. The study employed monthly time series data from July 2002 to March 2013, and the data were obtained from the South African Reserve Bank. The study employed a Vector Autoregression (VAR) model to run the results. The authors found out that oil prices and exchange rates have a positive relationship with inflation expectations in the long run. The food variable is inversely related to inflation expectations [31]. The study further indicated that oil, exchange rates, interest rates, and food costs are Granger causes of inflation expectations, both in the short run and long run. The study concluded that stable and low inflation together with well-anchored inflation expectations is important to monetary authorities as they help in achieving monetary policy objectives such as economic growth and financial stability.

This section laid down both the theoretical and empirical framework of the study. The first theory is the fiscal theory of the price level, which suggests that there is a need to understand that tax cuts and a rise in government spending do not necessarily have to be paid by higher taxes, and this may create too much unstable public debt [14]. Contrary to the first theory, the second theory is the Ricardian equivalence hypothesis, which does not consider the inflation expectations resulting from an increase in public debt [16]. The theory is based on the notion that a tax cut today is balanced by a rise in future taxes. In examining the empirical literature, more attention was given to taxation and inflation in most countries than the relationship between inflation expectations and taxation. Most studies reveal that there is a negative insignificant relationship between taxation and inflation. A relationship between public debt and taxation was found to be negative and that a stable relationship exists between public debt and inflation. Hence, this study will contribute by documenting new knowledge to the literature in addressing the impact of inflation expectations and public debt on taxation in South Africa.

3. Research methodology

3.1 The estimated model

The model used in this study is an econometric model, which runs multiple regression analyses between taxation as a dependent variable and the independent variables that affect taxation such as inflation expectations and public debt. Inflation (CPI) is a control variable in the model. The general model is specified as follows:

$$TAX = f(INFE, PD, CPI) \tag{1}$$

Eq. (1) describes the relationship between the dependent variable (taxation) and the independent variables (inflation expectations, public debt, and inflation rate). Where TAX is Taxation, INFE is Inflation expectations, PD is public debt, and CPI is Inflation.

3.2 Data

The study used quarterly secondary time series data obtained from the South African Reserve Bank. Due to the availability of data, especially for inflation expectations, the study covered the period from 2000 to 2020.

3.3 Estimation techniques

An ARDL-based ECM is employed in this study to analyze the short-run effects of inflation expectations and public debt on taxation. After testing for stationarity, if variables portray different orders of integration like at first level [I (0)] or at first differencing [I (1)], the ARDL can be employed [18, 32, 33]. The ARDL approach simultaneously captures the cointegration between a set of variables, the long-run and short-run estimates including the speed of adjustment. The ARDL cointegration test is also called the bounds test [33] and indicates if the long-run relationship exists in the series. It is advantageous due to its ability to incorporate small sample size data and yet generate valid results [32]. The ARDL bounds test gives the lower bound critical value and the upper bound critical value. If the computed F-statistics lie above the upper critical bounds test, we reject the null hypothesis of no cointegration, indicating that cointegration exists. In the case where the computed F-statistic lies in between the two bounds test, the cointegration becomes inconclusive [33]. When the F-statistics is below the lower bound, then there is no cointegration.

To determine the long-run estimates, the short-run dynamics, and ECM, Eq. (1) can be transformed into Eq. (2):

$$\begin{aligned}\Delta TAX_t = {} & \alpha + \sum_{i=1}^{k} \beta_1 \Delta TAX_{t-1} + \sum_{i=1}^{k} \beta_2 \Delta INFE_{t-1} + \sum_{i=1}^{k} \beta_3 \Delta PD_{t-1} \\ & + \sum_{i=1}^{k} \beta_4 \Delta LCPI_{t-1} + \delta_1 TAX_{t-1} + \delta_2 INFE_{t-1} + \delta_3 PD_{t-1} + \delta_4 CPI_{t-1} \\ & + \varphi ECM_{t-1} + \varepsilon_t \end{aligned} \tag{2}$$

Where Δ denotes the first difference operator in the model, α represents the constant, and ε represents the error term also known as the white noise disturbance. The long-run relationship in the model is represented by $\delta_1 - \delta_4$ coefficients. The short-run relationship in the model is represented by $\beta_1 - \beta_4$ coefficients, *phi* denotes the speed of adjustments, and ECM denotes the residual obtained from estimated cointegration in the equation. As Engle and Granger in 1987 put it, error-correcting or simply ECM allows long-run components of variables to obey equilibrium constraints while short-run components have a flexible dynamic specification [9, 18, 21]. After confirming the long-run equilibrium among the variables with the bounds test, the short-run, long-run and ECM coefficients (α, β's, δ, φ) are estimated using ARDL [21].

The study employs the Granger causality test to determine the nature of the relationship among the variables in the study. This study requires an assessment of whether these variables Granger cause each other and the nature of Granger causality if it is bidirectional (that is, the variables have an impact on each other) or unidirectional (only one variable has an impact on the other) or independent (they have no impact on each other) (Gujarati and Porter, 2003). The first variable is said to Granger cause the second if the forecast of the second variable improves when lagged values of the first variable are considered [28, 30].

3.4 Diagnostic and stability tests

The study conducted diagnostic tests for heteroskedasticity, serial correlation, and normality [7]. For heteroskedasticity, the study employed the Breusch-Pagan Godfrey test, for serial correlation the Breusch-Godfrey LM test, and Kurtosis for normality. The study utilized the cumulative sum of recursive residuals (CUSUM) and CUSUM-square to check the stability of the model [11].

4. Findings and discussions

The unit-roots results indicated that the variables are integrated at different orders, which are I (0) and I (1), hence the study is employing the ARDL bounds test. **Table 1** presents the results of the ARDL bounds test approach. The estimates were found using E-views 12, which automatically chose the optimal lag length for the model.

Table 1 shows significant levels for the lower bound and upper bound at 1%, 5%, and 10%. The number of independent variables understudy is 3, hence k = 3. The results show an F-statistic value of 8.51, which is greater than the lower bound I (0) and upper bound at all levels of significance (1%, 5%, 10%) respectively. The lower bound and the upper bound critical values are obtained from [33]. The information about F-statistics means that there is cointegration. The existence of cointegration in the model provides evidence of a long-run relationship between all the independent variables on taxation through the ARDL bounds test approach.

The cointegration results are consistent with prior expectations and other studies' findings that examined public debt, budget deficit, and tax policy reforms for fiscal consolidation in Sri Lanka [10]. In their study [10], they found a positive and statistically significant relationship between public debt and taxation. Additionally, other studies analyzed the relationship between taxation and inflation in Nigeria [9]. The study revealed that cointegration exists between the variables. It is therefore necessary to estimate the long-run and short-run coefficients and speed of adjustment, and **Table 2** indicates the results of ARDL estimates.

The results in **Table 2** show that there is a significant positive relationship between inflation expectations and taxation in South Africa. A unit change in inflation expectations will result in a 0.84 unit change in taxation (ceteris paribus) in the South African context. This relationship is statistically significant at a 1% level of significance. This is in line with economic theory, and the fiscal theory of price level because when consumers, as well as businesses, expect the inflation rate to rise in the future, this will increase their income tax, capital gains tax, and profits [14]. However, these findings differ from some studies that found a negative relationship though that study was between inflation expectation and aggregate demand [18].

The results further indicate that there is a negative significant relationship between public debt and taxation in South Africa as indicated in **Table 2**. The results show that when public debt increases by 1 unit, taxation will decline by 7.86 units (ceteris

Test statistics	Value	Significance	Lower bound	Upper bound
F-statistics	8.51			
		10%	2.2	3.09
		5%	2.65	3.49
		1%	3.29	4.37

Table 1.
ARDL bounds test computed from E-views 12.

Variable	Coefficients	Probability
Dependent Variable: Taxation		
Long-run results		
Inflation expectations	0.8386	0.0007
Public debt	−7.8686	0.0039
Inflation	0.0832	0.5076
Short-run results		
Speed of adjustment	−0.8267	0.0000
D (Inflation expectations)	0.0618	0.8943
D (Public debt)	1.5133	0.8272
D (Inflation)	−0.1796	0.0250
Constant	90.3247	0.0000

Table 2.
ARDL results computed from E-views 12.

paribus). Therefore, there is an inverse relationship between public debt and taxation. This relationship is statistically significant at a 1% level of significance. This inverse relationship can mean that when public debt increases, the government does not immediately finance its debt through taxation. They might borrow money from banking institutions or International Monetary Fund (IMF). The Ricardian equivalence theory confirms that when public debt increases, we should estimate that taxation will increase, but this does not occur immediately when public debt rises [15, 16]. Hence, in South Africa, the government does not finance its debt through taxation immediately when there is an increment in public debt. The results are in line with studies that found a negative significant relationship between public debt and taxation in the long run [10, 24]. Inflation as one of the control variables indicates a positive insignificant relationship between taxation.

In the short run, inflation is the only significant variable at 5% (see **Table 2**). The coefficient of the speed of adjustment is −0.83 implying that deviation from long-run inflation expectations and public debt in taxation is corrected by 83% of the following period. This means the system can adjust by fluctuating, and this fluctuation will decrease in each period and return to equilibrium. The speed of adjustment confirms the existence of a stable long-run relationship [23, 24]. **Table 3** displays the results of Granger causality to determine the direction the relationship that the series takes.

In **Table 3**, there is unidirectional causality between inflation expectations and taxation. Inflation expectations have a positive impact on taxation at a 1% level of significance. This leads to the rejection of the null hypothesis since a unidirectional relationship exists between inflation expectations and taxation. The results are like findings in the study by [27]. There is also a unidirectional relationship between taxation and public debt. Taxation Granger causes public debt at a 1% level of significance. This concedes with the findings of [28], who revealed that a unidirectional relationship exists between taxation and public debt in South Africa. The results further indicate that inflation Granger causes taxation; hence, there is a unidirectional relationship between inflation and taxation in South Africa. This coincides with the findings by [28].

Null hypothesis	Probability
Inflation expectation does not Granger cause taxation	0.0048
Taxation does not Granger cause inflation expectation	0.7055
Public debt does not Granger cause taxation	0.2698
Taxation does not Granger cause public debt	0.0011
Inflation does not Granger cause taxation	0.0016
Taxation does not Granger cause inflation	0.7524
Public debt does not Granger cause inflation expectation	0.2656
Inflation expectation does not Granger cause public debt	0.0236
Inflation does not Granger cause inflation expectation	6.E-06
Inflation expectation does not Granger cause inflation	0.3986
Inflation does not Granger cause public debt	0.0125
Public debt does not Granger cause inflation	0.1001

Table 3.
Granger causality computed from E-views 12.

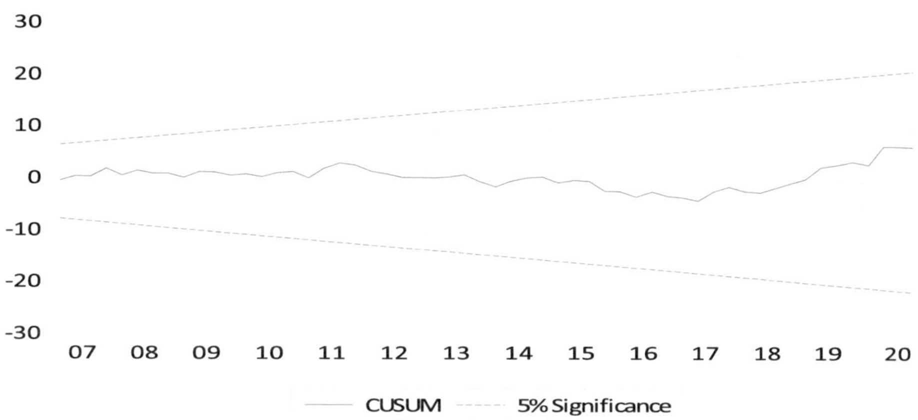

Figure 1.
CUSUM computed from E-views 12.

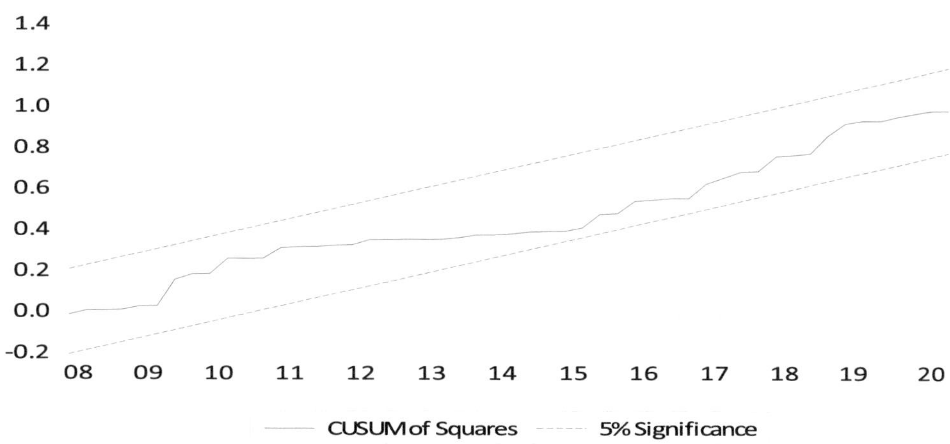

Figure 2.
CUSUM of squares computed from E-views 12.

The series was subjected to diagnostic and stability tests. All variables were free of heteroskedasticity and correlation as the probability of the variables was insignificant. The Kurtosis of 3.5 indicates that the series follows a normal distribution [18]. In addition, the CUSUM, as well as the CUSUM of squares, shows that the model is stable as illustrated in **Figures 1** and **2** by the blue line inside the red lines.

5. Conclusion and recommendations

The study investigated the relationship between inflation expectations and public debt on taxation, a proxy of personal income tax, capital gains tax, and profits in South Africa from 2000 quarter 3 to 2020 quarter 4. To achieve the objectives that are stated in Section 1, the study used secondary time series data gathered from the South African Reserve Bank. The ARDL and Granger causality methods have been employed in the analysis. To scrutinize the order of integration among the variables, the study used the Augmented Dickey-Fuller (ADF) test and Phillips Perron (PP).

The results revealed that there are different orders of integration since taxation, inflation expectations, and public debt are integrated at I (1) for both methods while inflation is integrated at I (0). Hence, the study adopted the ARDL techniques. The study found out that inflation expectations and public debts are the two main macro-economic variables that have an impact on taxation in South Africa, in the long run. The results revealed that there is a positive significant relationship between inflation expectations and taxation in the long run. However, the study found a negative correlation between public debt and taxation in the long run, but positively related in the short run. The pairwise Granger causality tests found that inflation expectations Granger cause taxation. There is a unidirectional relationship between inflation expectations and taxation. A causal relationship also existed from taxation to public debt.

Policymakers have long understood the importance of communication strategies and the importance of managing economic expectations; therefore, they must always communicate or inform economic participants (households and firms) about the changes in inflation expectations that might occur in the future. Using monetary policy tools can help policymakers to strive to anchor inflation expectations at roughly 3–6%, which is the inflation target rate in South Africa. This is to help inflation expectations to remain stable. There must be a balance between financing public debt through borrowing and taxation. An increase in taxation may place slow pressure on inflation, which will, in turn, enable the Reserve Bank to keep up with high-interest rates. Hence, there is a need for coordination between fiscal and monetary policies to achieve stability in the economy.

Conflict of interest

The authors declare no conflict of interest.

DOI: http://dx.doi.org/10.5772/intechopen.107389

Author details

Thobeka Ncanywa* and Noko Setati
Walter Sisulu University, Butterworth, South Africa

*Address all correspondence to: tncanywa@wsu.ac.za

References

[1] Mongale IP. The implications of labour productivity and labour costs on the South African economy. Journal of Reviews on Global Economics. 2019;**8**: 1298-1307

[2] Yellen JL. Inflation, uncertainty, and monetary policy. Business Economics. 2017;**52**(4):194-207

[3] Corsetti G, Dedola L. The mystery of the printing press: Monetary policy and self-fulfilling debt crises. Journal of the European Economic Association. 2016; **14**(6):1329-1371

[4] Kantor B. Recent monetary history: A monetarist perspective. Journal of Applied Corporate Finance. 2022;**34**(2): 82-99

[5] Bureau For Economic Research SU. Trends: August 2021. BER: Trends: Full Survey. 2021;**44**(8):10-102

[6] Rudd JB. Why do we think that inflation expectations matter for inflation? (and should we?). Review of Keynesian Economics. 2022;**10**(1):25-45

[7] Lopes da Veiga JA, Ferreira-Lopes A, Sequeira TN. Public debt, Economic growth and inflation in African economies. South African Journal of Economics. 2016;**84**(2):294-322

[8] Afonso A, Ibrahim Y. The macroeconomic effects of public debt: An empirical analysis of Mozambique. Applied Economics. 2020;**52**(2):212-226

[9] Obaretin O, Akhor SO. Taxation and inflation in Nigeria: An empirical analysis. 2019;**10**(4):91-98

[10] Vinayagathasan T, Ranjith JS. Public debt, budget deficit and tax policy reforms for fiscal consolidation in Sri Lanka: Rationale and feasibility. Sri Lanka Journal of Social Sciences. 2021; **44**(1):97-109

[11] Balcilar M, Chang S, Gupta R, Miller SM. The relationship between the inflation rate and inequality across the US states: A semiparametric approach. Quality & Quantity. 2018;**52**(5): 2413-2425

[12] Leibrandt-Loxton N. Agenda-setting as a tool of soft power in multilateral parliamentary diplomacy: Experiences of the south African parliament. South African Journal of International Affairs. 2022;**29**(1):69-90

[13] Yasmin F, Urooge S, Umair M, Ali S. Revisiting the dynamic impact of fiscal policy on inflation in Pakistan. Journal of Accounting and Finance in Emerging Economies. 2021;**7**(2):349-356

[14] Christiano L, Fitzgerald TJ. Understanding the fiscal theory of the price level. 2000;**7668**:9-31

[15] Afzal M. Ricardian equivalence hypothesis: Evidence from Pakistan. E3 Journal of Business Management and Economics. 2012;**3**(6):258-265

[16] Abel BA, Ben BS, Croushore D. Macroeconomics. 8th Global ed. Pearson UK: Prentice Hall; 2014

[17] Geronikolaou G, Spyromitros E, Tsintzos P. Progressive taxation and human capital as determinants of inflation persistence. Economic Modelling. 2020;**88**:82-97

[18] Ncanywa T, Ralarala O. The effects of expectation inflation on aggregate demand: Examining the south African inflation Expectation Channel of south

African monetary policy. Journal of Reviews on Global Economics. 2020;**9**: 437-445

[19] Mazhar U, Méon PG. Taxing the unobservable: The impact of the shadow economy on inflation and taxation. World Development. 2017;**90**: 89-103

[20] Atan JA. Tax policy, inflation and unemployment in Nigeria (1970–2008). European Journal of Business and Management. 2013;**5**(15):114-129

[21] Aimola AU, Odhiambo NM. Public debt and inflation nexus in Nigeria: An ARDL bounds test approach. Cogent Economics & Finance. 2021;**9**(1): 1921905

[22] Aimola AU, Odhiambo NM. Public debt and inflation: Empirical evidence from Ghana. Development Studies Research. 2021;**8**(1):1-3

[23] Ezirim CB, Mojekwu K, Amuzie AE, Muoghalu MI. The relationship between domestic public debt burden and inflationary pressures in Nigeria: Is there a causal relationship? International Journal of Business & Public Administration. 2016;**13**(2):80-98

[24] Anichebe AS. Implications of tax policy on inflation in Nigeria (1981-2012). Developing Country Studies. 2015;**5**(21):103-113

[25] Ezeji Chigbu E, Odinakachi NC. Taxation and the Nigerian economy: (1994-2012). Management Studies and Economic Systems. 2015;**2**(2):111-128

[26] Loganathan N, Ismail S, Streimikiene D, Hassan AA, Zavadskas EK, Mardani A. Tax reform, inflation, financial development and economic growth in Malaysia. ESPERA. 2017;**20**(4):152-165

[27] Adegbite TA, Azeez BA. The long run effect of interest rate and money supply on petroleum profit tax (PET) in Nigeria. IOSR Journal of Business and Management. 2015;**17**(1):18-26

[28] Radnia K, Rasoulpour Y. The granger causality of inflation rate, oil revenue and taxation in Iran. International Journal of Economics, Commerce and Management. 2015;**3**(10):130-144

[29] Yien LC, Abdullah H, Azam M. Granger causality analysis between inflation, debt and exchange rate: Evidence from Malaysia. International Journal of Academic Research in Accounting, Finance and Management Sciences. 2017;**7**(1):189-196

[30] Murshed M, Amin S, Chadni MH. Causality analysis between inflation, budget deficit and money supply: Empirical evidence from Bangladesh. World Journal of Social Sciences. 2018; **8**(3):94-109

[31] Sibanda K, Hove P, Murwirapachena G. Oil prices, exchange rates, and inflation expectations in South Africa. International Business & Economics Research Journal (IBER). 2015;**14**(4):587-602

[32] Nkoro E, Uko AK. Autoregressive distributed lag (ARDL) cointegration technique: Application and interpretation. Journal of Statistical and Econometric methods. 2016;**5**(4):63-91

[33] Pesaran MH, Shin Y, Smith RJ. Bounds testing approaches to the analysis of level relationships. Journal of Applied Econometrics. 2001;**16**(3): 289-326

Chapter 6

Incorporating Model Uncertainty in Market Response Models with Multiple Endogenous Variables by Bayesian Model Averaging

Jonathan Lee and Alex Lenkoski

Abstract

We develop a method to incorporate model uncertainty by model averaging in generalized linear models subject to multiple endogeneity and instrumentation. Our approach builds on a Gibbs sampler for the instrumental variable framework that incorporates model uncertainty in both outcome and instrumentation stages. Direct evaluation of model probabilities is intractable in this setting. However, we show that by nesting model moves inside the Gibbs sampler, a model comparison can be performed via conditional Bayes factors, leading to straightforward calculations. This new Gibbs sampler is slightly more involved than the original algorithm and exhibits no evidence of mixing difficulties. We further show how the same principle may be employed to evaluate the validity of instrumentation choices. We conclude with an empirical marketing study: estimating opening box office by three endogenous regressors (prerelease advertising, opening screens, and production budget).

Keywords: multiple endogeneity, instrumental variables, Bayesian model averaging, conditional Bayes factors, box office forecasting

1. Introduction

Market response modeling focuses on estimating the effects of marketing activities on performance. However, marketing managers are often strategic in their use of marketing activities and adapt them in response to factors unobserved by the researcher [1–3]. Endogeneity arises, for example, when a firm's marketing strategies such as advertising spending, channel selection, and pricing are nonrandom and influenced by the firm- and industry-level factors [4–6]. Strategic management decisions are endogenous to their expected effects on market performance. Therefore, empirical market response models that seek to estimate the causal effect of multiple marketing instruments need to account for such strategic planning of marketing activities, or otherwise may suffer from an endogeneity problem, leading to biased estimates of the effects of the marketing activities on performance [1, 3, 4, 7]. Dealing with endogeneity has been extensively discussed in the marketing literature, especially concerning different forms of regression and panel models [1, 5, 8–10], choice models [11, 12], endogeneity correction based on a control function approach [13, 14], as well as structural equations models [4]. However, little research addresses incorporating model uncertainty related to endogeneity in generalized linear models.

We consider the problem of incorporating instruments and covariate uncertainty into the Bayesian estimation of an instrumental variable (IV) regression system. The concepts of model uncertainty and model averaging have received widespread attention in the economics literature for the standard linear regression framework [15–18] and in generalized linear models [19–22]. For a good introduction to Bayesian model averaging (BMA), see [23]. Primarily, these frameworks do not directly address the case of multiple endogenous variables, and only recently has attention been paid to model uncertainty involving multiple endogenous variables. Unfortunately, the nested nature of IV estimation renders direct model comparison difficult. In the economics literature, this has led to several different approaches [24, 25]. Durlauf et al. [25] consider approximations of marginal likelihoods in a framework similar to two-stage least squares. Lenkoski et al. [16] continue this development with the two-stage Bayesian model averaging (2SBMA) methodology, which uses a framework developed by Kleibergen and Zivot [26] to propose a two-stage extension of the unit information prior [27]. Similar approaches in closely related models have been developed by [15, 28].

Koop et al. [29] developed a fully Bayesian methodology that does not utilize approximations to integrated likelihoods. They present a reversible jump Markov chain Monte Carlo (RJMCMC) algorithm [30], which extends the methodology of Holmes et al. [31]. The authors then show that the method can handle a variety of priors, including those of [32, 33], and [34]. However, the authors note that the direct application of RJMCMC leads to significant mixing difficulties and relies on a complicated model move procedure similar to simulated tempering to escape local model modes. There is a more straightforward and relatively general model search procedure. Madigan and York [35] proposed the Markov Chain Monte Carlo Model Composition (MC3) in which one applies the same idea of a Metropolis-Hastings step for model jumps from RJMCMC but in a simplified fashion.

We propose an alternative solution to this problem: Instrumental Variable Bayesian Model Averaging (IVBMA). Our method builds on a Gibbs sampler for the IV framework, extended from that discussed in Rossi et al. [36]. While direct model comparisons are intractable, we introduce the notion of a conditional Bayes factor (CBF), first discussed by Dickey and Gunel [37] and employed in a seemingly unrelated regression context by [31]. The CBF compares two models in a nested hierarchical system, conditional on parameters not influenced by the models under consideration. We show that the CBF for both outcome and instrumental equations is exceedingly straightforward to calculate and essentially reduces to the normalizing constants of a multivariate normal distribution.

Further, we note that our method can handle generalized linear mixed models with multiple endogenous variables in a straightforward fashion. This leads to a procedure in which model moves are embedded in a Gibbs sampler, which we term MC3-within-Gibbs. Based on this order of operations, IVBMA is only trivially more complicated than a Gibbs sampler that does not incorporate model uncertainty and thus appears to have limited issues regarding mixing. This feature is essential as it shows more complicated scenarios involving endogeneity, instrumentation, and model uncertainty can be handled within this framework, an important feature when constructing more involved Bayesian hierarchical models.

When working with a large system of equations subject to endogeneity and instrumentation, there is a natural concern that the instrument assumptions may not hold. A host of frequentist-type hypotheses has been proposed to examine the instrument conditions; the most familiar to applied researchers is the test of Sargan [38]. There have been, to our knowledge, no similar checks of instrument validity proposed in the Bayesian IV literature outside of the approximate method advocated in [16]. We offer a new verification of instrument validity, also based on CBFs, which appears to be the Bayesian analog of the Sargan test. This method can integrate seamlessly with the IVBMA framework and offers a check of instrument validity.

The article proceeds as follows. The basic framework we consider and the Gibbs sampler ignoring model uncertainty is discussed in Section 2. Section 3 reviews the concept of model uncertainty, introduces the notion of CBFs, and derives the conditional model probabilities used by IVBMA. In Section 4, we propose our method of assessing instrument validity. Section 5 presents empirical illustrations of the proposed model for predicting box office revenues. Lastly, we summarize and conclude with potential applications of the IVBMA approach.

2. The instrumental variable model with multiple endogenous variables

We consider the following classic linear system model with multiple endogenous variables:

$$Y_{ir} = \boldsymbol{U}_i^{(r)'} \boldsymbol{\beta}_r + \varepsilon_{ir}, \tag{1}$$

where $r \in \{1, \ldots, R\}$ denotes the R equations in the system and $i \in \{1, \ldots, n\}$ a set of *iid* observations. Throughout, we assume that Y_{i1} represents the dependent outcome of interest and $(Y_{i2}, \ldots, Y_{iR})$ represent endogenously determining variables for observation i. Thus, each covariate vector $\boldsymbol{U}_i^{(r)}$ has length p_r and is formed such that

$$\boldsymbol{U}_i^{(1)} = \left(Y_{i1} \ldots Y_{iR} W_{i1} \ldots W_{iq}\right)^{\prime},$$

while

$$\boldsymbol{U}_i^{(r)} = \left(Z_{i1} \ldots Z_{is} W_{i1} \ldots W_{iq}\right)',$$

for $r > 1$. Letting $\varepsilon_i = (\varepsilon_{i1}, \ldots, \varepsilon_{iR})'$, we assume

$$\boldsymbol{\varepsilon}_i \sim \mathcal{N}_R\left(0, \boldsymbol{K}^{-1}\right). \tag{2}$$

When $K_{1r} \neq 0$ for a given $r > 1$, this implies a lack of conditional independence between the residuals for the response and the associated endogenous variable. This contaminates inference if unaccounted for, necessitating the existence of instruments $\boldsymbol{Z}_i$ that do not appear in $\boldsymbol{U}_i^{(1)}$ and joint estimation of the parameters in Eq. (1) and Eq. (2).

Generalized linear mixed models provide a unified approach that directly acknowledges multiple levels of dependency and model different data types [39–42]. Extensions to generalized linear models implicitly assume a continuous response with

Gaussian errors. Extending these developments to alternative sampling models is straightforward in the context of a random-effects framework. Let g a link function such that for the response Y_i,

$$E[Y_{i1}] = g^{-1}\left(\boldsymbol{U}_i^{(1)'}\boldsymbol{\beta}_1 + \varepsilon_{i1}\right), \tag{3}$$

while the remaining Y_{ir} have forms given by Eq. (1), and the residual vector remains distributed according to a $\mathcal{N}(0, \boldsymbol{K}^{-1})$ distribution. Below we first develop the normal IVBMA with an identity link.

We proceed by discussing the Bayesian estimation of these parameters under standard conjugate priors, following the developments of [36]. Accordingly, with each parameter vector, we assume

$$\boldsymbol{\beta}_r \sim \mathcal{N}(0, \mathbb{I}_{p_r}),$$

and

$$\boldsymbol{K} \sim \mathcal{W}(3, \mathbb{I}_R)$$

where $\boldsymbol{K} \sim \mathcal{W}(\delta, \boldsymbol{D})$ represents a Wishart distribution with density

$$pr(\boldsymbol{K}|\delta, \boldsymbol{D}) \propto |\boldsymbol{K}|^{\frac{\delta-2}{2}} exp\left(-\frac{1}{2}tr(\boldsymbol{KD})\right)\mathbf{1}_{K\in\mathbb{P}_R},$$

where $\mathbb{P}_R$ is the cone of symmetric positive definite matrices.

Let $\boldsymbol{\theta} = \{\boldsymbol{\beta}_1, \dots, \boldsymbol{\beta}_R, \boldsymbol{K}\}$ represent the collection of parameters to be estimated. Denote the data $\mathcal{D} = \{\boldsymbol{Y}, \boldsymbol{U}^{(1)}, \dots, \boldsymbol{U}^{(R)}\}$, where $\boldsymbol{Y}$ is the $n \times R$ matrix of responses and endogenous variables, and each $\boldsymbol{U}^{(r)}$ is a $n \times p_r$ matrix. Then, our goal is to determine the posterior distribution $pr(\boldsymbol{\theta}|\mathcal{D})$. Rossi et al. [36] discuss the estimation of this model for the case when $R = 2$ and note that it is not possible to evaluate this posterior directly. However, an approximate inference may be performed via Gibbs sampling.

Fix r and suppose that $\boldsymbol{K}$ and all $\boldsymbol{\beta}_t$ for $t \neq r$ are given. Note, by properties of standard normal variates that

$$\varepsilon_{ir}|\boldsymbol{K},\{\boldsymbol{\beta}_t\}_{t\neq r} \sim \mathcal{N}\left(\mu_{ir}, K_{rr}^{-1}\right),$$

where

$$\mu_{ir} = -\sum_{t\neq r}\frac{K_{rt}}{K_{rr}}\left(Y_{it} - \boldsymbol{U}_i^{(t)}\boldsymbol{\beta}_t\right).$$

Set $\tilde{Y}_{ir} = Y_{ir} - \mu_{ir}$ and thus note that

$$\tilde{Y}_{ir} \sim \mathcal{N}\left(\boldsymbol{U}_i^{(r)}\boldsymbol{\beta}_r, K_{rr}^{-1}\right).$$

The act of conditioning, therefore, turns the original system into a simple linear regression problem, and via standard results, we have that

$$\boldsymbol{\beta}_r|\boldsymbol{K},\{\boldsymbol{\beta}_t\}_{t\neq r} \sim \mathcal{N}\left(\hat{\boldsymbol{\beta}}_r, \boldsymbol{\Omega}_r^{-1}\right) \tag{4}$$

where

$$\boldsymbol{\Omega}_r = K_{rr}\boldsymbol{U}^{(r)'}\boldsymbol{U}^{(r)} + \mathbb{I}_{p_r},$$

$$\hat{\boldsymbol{\beta}}_r = K_{rr}\boldsymbol{\Omega}_r^{-1}\boldsymbol{U}^{(r)'}\tilde{\boldsymbol{Y}}_r.$$

Finally, suppose that all $\boldsymbol{\beta}_r$ are given, then

$$\boldsymbol{K} \sim \mathcal{W}(\delta + \boldsymbol{n}, \boldsymbol{E} + \mathbb{I}_R), \tag{5}$$

where

$$\boldsymbol{E} = \sum_{i=1}^{n} \boldsymbol{\varepsilon}_i \boldsymbol{\varepsilon}_{i'},$$

with each $\boldsymbol{\varepsilon}_i$ computed relative to the current state of $\boldsymbol{\beta}_1, \dots, \boldsymbol{\beta}_R$.

Eq. (4) and Eq. (5) thereby give the full conditionals necessary for the Gibbs sampler. For a basic introduction to MCMC sampling with illustration, see [43]. Our approach differs slightly from that of Rossi et al. [36], in that their Gibbs sampler features a more involved manner of updating the instrumental covariates $\boldsymbol{\beta}_2$. Though the two approaches evaluate the same posterior distribution, the application of [36] when $R \geq 3$ is not straightforward, and it only applies to a linear regression model. Therefore, we find that the above approach leads to more coherent implementation and description, and therefore prefer it to that of [36] for the generalized linear models with multiple endogenous variables.

For a Poisson regression using a log link in Eq. (3), the term ε_{i1} is no longer observable and is often referred to as a Poisson random effect model [41, 44, 45]. However, in a Gibbs sampling framework, these factors may be incorporated into additional parameters to be determined in the posterior. Appendix 2 shows how MCMC methods can be implemented when Y_{i1} in (3) has a Poisson likelihood.

3. Incorporating model uncertainty

We outline our method for incorporating model uncertainty into the framework in Eq. (1) and Eq. (2). To explain the motivation behind our CBF approach, we first review a classic Bayesian model selection method. We then show how the concept of Bayes Factors can be usefully embedded in a Gibbs sampler yielding CBFs. These CBFs are then shown to yield straightforward calculations.

3.1 Model selection and Bayes factors

In a general framework, incorporating model uncertainty involves considering a collection of candidate models $\mathcal{I}$, using the data $\mathcal{D}$. Each model I consists of a collection of probability distributions for the data $\mathcal{D}$, $\{pr(\mathcal{D}|\psi), \psi \in \Psi_I\}$ where Ψ_I denotes the parameter space for the parameters of model I and is a subset of the full parameter space Ψ.

By letting the model become an additional parameter to be assessed in the posterior, we aim to calculate the posterior model probabilities given the data $\mathcal{D}$. By Bayes' rule

$$pr(I|\mathcal{D}) = \frac{pr(\mathcal{D}|I)pr(I)}{\sum_{I' \in \mathcal{I}} pr(\mathcal{D}|I')pr(I')} \tag{6}$$

where $pr(I)$, denotes the prior probability for model $I \in \mathcal{I}$.

The integrated likelihood $pr(\mathcal{D}|I)$, is defined by

$$pr(\mathcal{D}|I) = \int_{\Psi_I} pr(\mathcal{D}|\psi)pr(\psi|I)d\psi \tag{7}$$

where $pr(\psi|I)$ is the prior for ψ under model I, which by definition has all its mass on Ψ_I.

One possibility for pairwise comparison of models is offered by the Bayes factor (BF), which is in most cases defined together with the posterior odds [22, 46]. The posterior odds of model I versus model I' are given by

$$\frac{pr(I|\mathcal{D})}{pr(I'|\mathcal{D})} = \frac{pr(\mathcal{D}|I)}{pr(\mathcal{D}|I')} \frac{pr(I)}{pr(I')},$$

where

$$\frac{pr(\mathcal{D}|I)}{pr(\mathcal{D}|I')} \text{and} \frac{pr(I)}{pr(I')}$$

denote the Bayes factor and the prior odds of I versus I', respectively.

When the integrated likelihood in Eq. (7) and thus the BF can be computed directly, a straightforward method for exploring the model space, Markov Chain Monte Carlo Model Composition (MC3), was developed by Madigan and York [35]. MC3 determines posterior model probabilities by generating a stochastic process that moves through the model space $\mathcal{I}$ and has equilibrium distribution $pr(I|\mathcal{D})$. Given the current state $I^{(s)}$, MC3 (a) proposes a new model I' according to a proposal distribution $q(\cdot|\cdot)$, (b) calculates

$$\alpha = \frac{pr(\mathcal{D}|I')pr(I')q\left(I^{(s)}|I'\right)}{pr\left(\mathcal{D}|I^{(s)}\right)pr\left(I^{(s)}\right)q\left(I'|I^{(s)}\right)},$$

and (c) sets $I^{(s+1)} = I'$ with probability $\min\{\alpha, 1\}$, otherwise setting $I^{(s+1)} = I^{(s)}$. It is important to note that moving between models via the MC3 approach constitutes a valid MCMC transition. This feature is critical in the development below, in that MC3 moves may be nested inside larger structures in a manner similar to Gibbs updates.

3.2 Model determination

Incorporating model uncertainty into the system Eq. (1) involves considering a separate model space $\mathcal{M}_r$ for each equation in the system. A given model $M_r \in \mathcal{M}_r$ thus restricts certain elements of $\boldsymbol{\beta}_r$ to zero, and we write $\boldsymbol{\beta}_{M_r}$ to indicate the non-zero elements according to M_r. We further let Λ_{M_r} be the subspace of $\mathbb{R}^{p_r}$ spanned by $\boldsymbol{\beta}_{M_r}$. Ideally, we would be able to incorporate model uncertainty into this system in a manner analogous to that described above. Unfortunately, the following cannot be directly calculated in any discernible way.

$$pr(\mathcal{D}|M_1, \ldots M_R) = \int_{\mathbb{P}_R}\int_{\Lambda_{M_1}}\cdots\int_{\Lambda_{M_R}} pr\left(\mathcal{D}|\{\boldsymbol{\beta}_{M_r}\}_{r=1}^{R}, \boldsymbol{K}\right)pr(\boldsymbol{K})\prod_{r=1}^{R} pr(\boldsymbol{\beta}_{M_r})d\boldsymbol{\beta}_{M_1}\cdots d\boldsymbol{\beta}_{M_R}d\boldsymbol{K}$$

Therefore, an implementation of MC3 in the product space of $\mathcal{M}_1 \times \cdots \times \mathcal{M}_R$ is infeasible. What we show below, however, is that embedding MC3 within the Gibbs sampler, and therefore calculation using CBFs to move between models offers an extremely efficient solution. CBFs were initially discussed in Dickey and Gunel [37] in a different context.

Given the system Eq. (1), fix r and suppose that $\boldsymbol{\theta}_{-r} = \left\{\boldsymbol{K}, \{\boldsymbol{\beta}_t\}_{t\neq r}\right\}$ is given. Now consider comparing two models $M_r, L_r \in \mathcal{M}_r$. Finally, suppose that the prior over models $\mathcal{M}_r$ is set independent of $\boldsymbol{\theta}_{-r}$. We then have

$$\frac{pr(M_r|\mathcal{D}, \boldsymbol{\theta}_{-r})}{pr(L_r|\mathcal{D}, \boldsymbol{\theta}_{-r})} = \frac{pr(\mathcal{D}|M_r, \boldsymbol{\theta}_{-r})}{pr(\mathcal{D}|L_r, \boldsymbol{\theta}_{-r})} \times \frac{pr(M_r)}{pr(L_r)}. \tag{8}$$

Thus, the conditional posterior odds depend on calculating a Bayes factor conditional on the current state of $\boldsymbol{\theta}_{-r}$.

Calculating the relevant terms in Eq. (6) is straightforward. In particular, we note that

$$pr(\mathcal{D}|M_r, \boldsymbol{\theta}_{-r}) = \int_{\Lambda_{M_r}} pr(\mathcal{D}|\boldsymbol{\beta}_{M_r}, \boldsymbol{\theta}_{-r})pr(\boldsymbol{\beta}_{M_r}|M_r)d\boldsymbol{\beta}_{M_r},$$

which is, in essence, an integrated likelihood for model M_r conditional on fixed values of $\boldsymbol{\theta}_{-r}$. In Appendix 1, we show that

$$\int_{\Lambda_{M_r}} pr(\mathcal{D}|\boldsymbol{\beta}_{M_r}, \boldsymbol{\theta}_{-r})d\beta_{M_r} \propto |\boldsymbol{\Omega}_{M_r}|^{-1/2} exp\left(\frac{1}{2}\hat{\boldsymbol{\beta}}_{M_r}{}'\boldsymbol{\Omega}_{M_r}\hat{\boldsymbol{\beta}}_{M_r}\right) \tag{9}$$

where $\hat{\boldsymbol{\beta}}_{M_r}$ and $\boldsymbol{\Omega}_{M_r}$ relative to the subspace Λ_{M_r}.

The power of this result is that the model M_r and the associated parameter $\boldsymbol{\beta}_{M_r}$ may then be updated in a block. In particular, we note that

$$pr(\boldsymbol{\beta}_r, M_r|\boldsymbol{\theta}_{-r}, \mathcal{D}) = pr(\boldsymbol{\beta}_r|M_r, \boldsymbol{\theta}_{-r}, \mathcal{D}) \times pr(M_r|\boldsymbol{\theta}_{-r}, \mathcal{D}).$$

Since MC3 constitutes a valid MCMC transition in the model space $\mathcal{M}_r$, we may first attempt to update M_r via Eq. (8) and then subsequently resample β_{M_r} via Eq. (4). By cycling through all R equations in Eq. (1) in this manner, and then subsequently updating $\boldsymbol{K}$, we have proposed a computationally efficient estimation strategy for incorporating model uncertainty in IV frameworks.

4. Assessing instrument validity

For the estimates $\boldsymbol{\beta}_1$ to have appropriate inferential properties, it is critical that the instrumental variables $\boldsymbol{Z}$ be valid. In other words, $E[\boldsymbol{Z}_i{}'\varepsilon_{i1}|\varepsilon_{i2}, \ldots, \varepsilon_{iR}] = \boldsymbol{0}$. Many tools exist for evaluating the validity of this assumption in frequentist settings, and the most popular method is the test of Sargan [38]. To our knowledge, consideration of similar assessments in a Bayesian framework has not been explored beyond the approximate analysis proposed in [16]. We offer a Bayesian evaluation of instrument validity, borrowing many of the ideas above and merging them with the idea of the Sargan test.

Suppose that all residuals were known. Let $\boldsymbol{\varsigma}$ be such that

$$\varsigma_i = \varepsilon_{i1} + \sum_{r=2}^{R} \frac{K_{1r}}{K_{11}} \varepsilon_{ir}.$$

The essential notion of the Sargan test is to consider the model,

$$\varsigma_i = \mathbf{Z}'_i \boldsymbol{\xi} + \eta_i, \eta_i \sim \mathcal{N}(0, \tau^{-1})$$

and test whether $\boldsymbol{\xi} \neq \mathbf{0}$. The mechanics of the Sargan test ultimately rely on asymptotic theory, and Lenkoski et al. [16] discuss its poor performance in low sample size environments.

Our approach is to model this in a Bayesian context. In particular, we consider two models: J_0 which states that $\boldsymbol{\xi} = \mathbf{0}$ and J_1 which puts $\boldsymbol{\xi} \in \mathbb{R}^q$. We then aim to determine whether $pr(J_0|\mathcal{D})$ is large, indicating instrument validity. Note that this can be represented as the following marginalization

$$pr(J_0|\mathcal{D}) = \int pr(J_0|\boldsymbol{\varsigma}, \mathcal{D}) pr(\boldsymbol{\varsigma}|\mathcal{D}) d\boldsymbol{\varsigma}. \tag{10}$$

Let $\left\{\boldsymbol{\theta}^{(1)}, \ldots, \boldsymbol{\theta}^{(S)}\right\}$ be an MCMC sample of $pr(\boldsymbol{\theta}|\mathcal{D})$ and $\{\varsigma^{(1)}, \ldots, \varsigma^{(S)}\}$ be the associated realization from each MCMC draw. This draw then enables us to approximate (10) with

$$\int pr(J_0|\varsigma, \mathcal{D}) pr(\varsigma|\mathcal{D}) d\varsigma = \frac{1}{S} \sum_{s=1}^{S} pr\left(J_0|\varsigma^{(s)}, \mathcal{D}\right).$$

Note that

$$pr\left(J_0|\varsigma^{(s)}, \mathcal{D}\right) = \frac{1}{1 + \frac{pr(J_1|\varsigma^{(s)}, \mathcal{D})}{pr(J_0|\varsigma^{(s)}, \mathcal{D})}}$$

and therefore, we have reduced the problem of assessing $pr(J_0|\mathcal{D})$ to evaluating several CBFs. At this juncture, note that

$$pr\left(J_0|\varsigma^{(s)}, \mathcal{D}\right) \propto pr\left(\varsigma^{(s)}|J_0, \mathcal{D}\right) \bullet pr(J_0) = \int_0^\infty pr\left(\varsigma^{(s)}|\tau, \mathcal{D}\right) pr(\tau) d\tau \bullet pr(J_0),$$

while

$$pr\left(J_1|\varsigma^{(s)}, \mathcal{D}\right) \propto pr\left(\varsigma^{(s)}|J_1, \mathcal{D}\right) \bullet pr(J_1) = \int_0^\infty \int_{\mathbb{R}^q} pr\left(\varsigma^{(s)}|\tau, \boldsymbol{\xi}, \mathcal{D}\right) pr(\boldsymbol{\xi}, \tau) d\boldsymbol{\xi} d\tau \bullet pr(J_1).$$

Evaluation of these integrals thus requires the specification of priors $pr(\tau)$ under J_0 and $pr(\boldsymbol{\xi}, \tau)$ under J_1 . Under the model J_0, we propose the standard prior

$$\tau \sim \Gamma(1/2, 1/2)$$

which yields

$$pr\left(J_0|\varsigma^{(s)}, \mathcal{D}\right) \propto \left(\frac{1}{2} + \frac{\varsigma^{(s)'}\varsigma^{(s)}}{2}\right)^{-(n+1)/2}. \tag{11}$$

For J_1, we use the prior

$$\tau \sim \Gamma(1/2, 1/2)$$
$$\boldsymbol{\xi}|\tau \sim \mathcal{N}\left(0, \tau^{-1}\mathbb{I}_q\right)$$

which yields

$$pr\left(J_1|\varsigma^{(s)}, \mathcal{D}\right) \propto |\Xi|^{-\frac{1}{2}}\left(\frac{1}{2} + \frac{\left(\varsigma^{(s)} - \mathbf{Z}\hat{\boldsymbol{\xi}}^{(s)}\right)'\left(\varsigma^{(s)} - \mathbf{Z}\hat{\boldsymbol{\xi}}^{(s)}\right)}{2}\right)^{-\frac{n+1}{2}}, \tag{12}$$

where

$$\Xi = \tau\left(\mathbf{Z}'\mathbf{Z} + \mathbb{I}_q\right),$$
$$\hat{\boldsymbol{\xi}} = \tau\Xi^{-1}\mathbf{Z}\varsigma^{(s)}.$$

This approach offers similar performance to the Sargan test, which has the desirable feature that it is a fully Bayesian approach, as opposed to the approximate test of [16], and it can be directly embedded in the Gibbs sampling procedures outlined above. We emphasize in the discussion section that further work can be done on this diagnostic.

5. Empirical study: determinants of opening box office

In this section, we consider a generalized linear model with an identity link in the presence of multiple endogenous variables and covariates based on the IVBMA framework incorporating model uncertainty. Based on previous studies of box office revenues, we estimate the effects of three endogenous predictors, prelaunch advertising spending, the number of screens, and production budget with other covariates on opening box office.

Several studies have established a significant link between advertising expenditures and box-office grosses [47–50]. Almost 90% of a movie's advertising budget is allocated in the weeks leading up to the theatrical launch [49] shows the importance of prerelease advertising. The number of screens on which a movie is released has been recognized as one of the most significant factors related to the box office [51–53]. Prerelease advertising spending and the number of opening screens need to be considered endogenous because it is plausible for movies that are expected to generate high box office gross to receive more advertising and distribution. That is, advertising spending and distribution are more likely to be determined by expected box office revenues.

Major studios dominate the movie marketplace regarding film production and distribution. The production budget is an essential predictor because big budgets translate into the casting of top actors and directors, lavish sets and costumes, special effects, and expensive digital manipulations, leading to heightened audience attractiveness [54, 55]. Previous studies [55–57] used production budget as a direct influencer or moderating variable, but it is also the studio's strategic decision using knowledge about viewers and competitors' actions, that is, the data reflect firm's strategic behavior [58]. While researchers examined endogeneity in advertising responsiveness using a control function approach [14] or price endogeneity using Gaussian copula [9], they did not simultaneously control for multiple endogenous variables or incorporate model uncertainty. The proposed approach can test the effects of three endogenous variables in a generalized framework.

5.1 Description of the data

Starting from all movies released by major studios from 2006 to 2007, we analyzed 130 movies, including 16 animation and 50 R-rated movies, based on the IMDb database. We have excluded films without the complete prerelease advertising information from TNS Media Intelligence. Advertising data include the total dollar value of prerelease media expenditure across 17 different media. The number of opening screens, production budget, and opening box office gross are obtained from IMDb.c om and BoxOfficeMojo.com. **Table 1** shows the summary statistics of the dependent variable and three endogenous variables. Opening box office gross varies from less than a million to over 100 million dollars. The production budget represents the most significant expense for movie studios [49]. For movies in our sample, they are about $52 million on average and vary from $4 million to $210 million. It becomes crucial for films with high production costs to succeed at the box office to recover their costs, resulting in higher advertising spending and showing at more theaters.

The three endogenous predictors were regressed on eleven potential instruments and thirteen additional covariates, summarized in **Table 2**. Covariates such as genre, MPAA rating, animation, sequels, and release date are publicly available on IMDb and The Numbers. The genre is classified into seven categories (action, comedy, drama, horror, Sci-Fi, mystery/suspense, and romance), and the MPAA rating into two dummy variables (R, PG-13, and others).

The MPAA rating is related to the potential size of viewers. Not R-rated movies are open to more moviegoers from the outset, making it necessary to have wider releases and intensive advertising. Critics' ratings are obtained from the Rotten Tomatoes website, which gives a composite score of 1–100 based on evaluations from movie critics. A monthly seasonality index was obtained by estimating a decomposition model using a time series of monthly box office gross. The seasonal parameter was optimized at 0.56 with the mean absolute percentage error of 10.5%.

	Mean	Median	SD	Range
Opening box office	20.48	14.32	17.90	(0.72, 102.75)
Prerelease advertising	4.39	4.16	2.17	(0.69, 10.79)
Number of opening screens	2729	2692	707	(825, 4054)
Production budget	52.15	35.0	44.21	(4, 210)

Table 1.
Summary statistics.

Instrumental variables (Z)	Release time	Period indicator based on 10-year box office gross
		(1 = May, June, July, December/0 = other months)
	Expert	Marketability ratings of industry experts
	Direct	Production and distribution by the same company
	Distributor	Production studio dummy variables (SD1–SD6)
		(1 = FOX, 2 = COLUMBIA, 3 = WARNER BROTHERS, 4 = UNIVERSAL, 5 = PARAMOUNT, 6 = DREAMWORKS, 7 = Others)
Covariates (W)	Seasonality	Seasonal index by decomposition model
	Sequels	Dummy variable
	Animation	Animation movies
	Critics review	Movie ratings from Rotten Tomatoes (0–100 points)
	GD1–GD7	Genre dummy variables
		(1 = action/adventure, 2 = comedy, 3 = drama, 4 = horror, 5 = Sci-Fi, 6 = mystery/suspense, 7 = romance, 8 = others)
	RD1–RD2	MPAA rating dummy variables
		(1 = R, 2 = PG13, 3 = Others)

Table 2.
Description of the instruments (Z) and covariates (W).

For the two endogenous variables, prerelease advertising and opening number of screens, we have used four common instruments of the 11 variables: (a) movie distributors, (b) release time, (c) average marketability ratings by three industry experts in one of the major studios, and (d) whether the same studio did production and distribution. Studios have considerable discretion over the amount and schedule of prelaunch advertising they allocate to each movie [51]. Because advertising elasticities for motion pictures are significantly higher compared to other industries [52], studios' decisions on prerelease advertising spending and opening screens would have a significant impact on the success at the box office. We have included eight major studios to examine any studio-specific effects on advertising and distribution. Release time is another critical characteristic since movie advertising is seasonal, as heavily supported movies are usually released in peak seasons [51]. Based on the monthly box office gross from 2001 to 2010, we have found a substantial increase in box office gross in May–July and December. A dummy variable is used to indicate those months. For the third endogenous variable, production budget, we exclude release time and expert ratings since they are unavailable at the time of budget decision. Similarly, the seasonal index and critics review were also excluded from the regression of the production budget. Some major studios like 20th Century Fox and Paramount are vertically integrated, having their distribution division. A dummy variable *Direct* indicates whether both production and distribution divisions finance a movie. For the common instruments on each endogenous regressor, the proposed IVBMA approach has a built-in capability of variable selection using the posterior inclusion probability.

5.2 Results

Table 3 shows the IVBMA posterior estimates of the first stage. The sum of the models' posterior probabilities containing the variable is called the inclusion probability [16, 23]. In **Table 3**, column *IncProb* shows posterior inclusion probabilities in the first stage, which provide a direct interpretation of the efficacy of an instrumentation strategy. Related to prerelease advertising spending, we find a robust movie-type effect for animation, sequels, and PG-13. Animated family films have performed consistently well at the box office, and Pixar and DreamWorks Animation are the most represented studios. Movie sequels build on the original movies' commercial success and can be considered a brand extension of the experiential product [59]. Given the original movie's brand power, a sequel usually achieves box office success [60]. The negative coefficient of *Sequels* results from relatively low advertising costs, which is one of the benefits of brand extensions [61]. The posterior inclusion probabilities of *Animation* and *Sequels* are 0.9, which shows generous production budgets for those movies. The marketability ratings by industry experts are significant predictors for prerelease advertising and opening screens. Considering that the ratings are based on the feedback from advance movie screenings, they are reliable indicators of box office performance accompanied by heavy advertising and broader release.

As expected, a seasonal index shows a high inclusion probability for both endogenous variables, which aligns with the common belief that movies with high expected gross are carefully scheduled to be released in peak seasons. *Release time*, however, shows no impact, and the result is mainly due to the sample characteristic that more than 65% of the movies in the sample were released in historically no peak months. Note that a seasonal index is calculated for the duration under investigation (2006–2007) while *Release time* is based on a 10-year window. Therefore, a seasonal index captures short-term fluctuations more accurately.

For prerelease advertising, the PG-13 rating is included with probability one. It concerns the size of potential viewers since non-R ratings imply greater reach among moviegoers, which may result in a higher level of advertising. There is empirical evidence from more than one systematic investigation to show that R-rated movies generate smaller revenues than those with less restrictive ratings [47, 62]. We also find that a dummy variable GD5 for Horror films is a significant predictor of prerelease advertising. This result may reflect the popular trend at that time. There are 15 horror movies in the sample including *I am Legend*, *Silent Hills*, and *Saw III*, which have been very successful at the box office. Consistent with previous literature on critics' reviews [49, 63], we find a significant impact of reviews on movie advertising. The industry practice of using critics' quotations in film advertisements supports the continuing authority of film critics. The use of critics' reviews in movie advertisements indicates distributors' beliefs and the significance of critics as a cultural intermediary for audiences [64].

In contrast, critical reviews were not included in explaining opening screens. It is consistent with the findings that the relationship between reviews and distributor's decision is spurious [65], and there is only a positivity bias of exhibitors such that an excellent review allows a movie to stay longer on-screen while negative reviews do not shorten a film's run [66]. That is, critical reviews do not influence an exhibitor's decision to keep or withdraw a movie from a theater.

As shown in **Table 3**, regarding production budget, distributor effects are evident from the high inclusion probabilities of the studios besides movie characteristics such as *Sequels* and *Animation*. Though 21st Century Fox and Columbia have released more

DOI: http://dx.doi.org/10.5772/intechopen.108927

	Prerelease advertising			Opening screens			Production budget		
	IncProb	Mean	Quantile	IncProb	Mean	Quantile	IncProb	Mean	Quantile
Intercept	0.436	−0.130	(−1.437, 0.872)	0.542	0.356	(−0.908, 2.189)	1	16.496	(16.037, 16.909)
Sequels	1	−0.415	(−0.480, −0.348)	0.201	0.025	(0, 0.211)	0.909	0.491	(0, 0.914)
Animation	1	0.197	(0.133, 0.266)	0.365	0.061	(0, 0.296)	0.901	0.562	(0, 1.083)
Seasonal index	1	1.418	(1.004, 1.836)	0.817	0.745	(0, 1.727)			
Critics review	1	1.111	(1.037, 1.184)	0.070	0	(−0.025, 0.032)			
R	0.089	0.004	(0, 0.068)	0.853	−0.139	(−0.288, 0)	0.242	0.041	(−0.123, 0.445)
PG-13	1	0.511	(0.467, 0.564)	0.189	−0.017	(−0.174, 0)	0.964	0.436	(0, 0.791)
Action/adventure	0.026	0	(0, 0)	0.055	0.001	(0, 0.029)	0.987	0.494	(0.183, 0.771)
Comedy	0.048	−0.002	(−0.033, 0)	0.062	0.002	(0, 0.038)	0.539	0.181	(0, 0.631)
Drama	0.048	0.001	(0, 0.030)	0.903	−0.149	(−0.259, 0)	0.168	−0.009	(−0.225, 0.124)
Horror	1	−0.229	(−0.289, −0.169)	0.081	−0.004	(−0.084, 0)	0.446	−0.139	(−0.595, 0)
Sci-Fi	0.062	0.003	(0, 0.051)	0.102	−0.006	(−0.112, 0)	0.202	0.017	(−0.178, 0.331)
Mystery/suspense	0.057	0.002	(0, 0.035)	0.046	0	(0, 0)	0.212	0.036	(−0.004, 0.358)
Romance	0.095	−0.005	(−0.068, 0)	0.125	−0.011	(−0.150, 0)	0.316	−0.085	(−0.600, 0.046)
Direct	0.028	0	(0, 0)	0.093	0.005	(0, 0.087)	0.724	0.222	(0, 0.543)
Fox	0.999	−0.147	(−0.203, −0.090)	0.065	0	(−0.025, 0.015)	0.219	0.021	(−0.196, 0.383)
Columbia	0.028	0	(0, 0)	0.074	−0.002	(−0.057, 0.003)	0.724	0.331	(0, 0.838)
Paramount	0.030	0	(0, 0)	0.114	0.009	(0, 0.134)	0.994	0.725	(0.311, 1.124)
Universal	0.034	0	(0, 0)	0.072	0.003	(0, 0.077)	0.885	0.488	(0, 0.943)
Warner Brothers	0.053	0.002	(0, 0.036)	0.071	−0.001	(−0.041, 0.020)	0.987	0.712	(0.253, 1.144)
MGM	0.038	0.001	(0, 0)	0.089	0.005	(0, 0.118)	0.249	0.053	(−0.088, 0.504)
Lions Gate	1	−0.421	(−0.498, −0.343)	0.404	−0.073	(−0.314, 0)	0.948	−0.676	(−1.161, 0)
Buena Vista	0.040	0	(0, 0)	0.092	0	(−0.051, 0.057)	0.208	0.008	(−0.262, 0.348)
Expert	1	2.134	(1.886, 2.449)	1	1.596	(1.139, 1.947)			
Release Time	0.026	0	(0, 0)	0.068	0.002	(0, 0.054)			

Table 3.
IVBMA results (first stage).

movies than other studios (37 in the sample), Paramount, Universal, and Warner Brothers had a higher average production budget per movie among major studios, and Lions Gate was the leading independent producer/distributor from 2006 to 2007. PG-13 rating, combined with the Action/Adventure genre consistently performs better than others at the box office by broadening its audience appeal [47]. Interestingly, the instrument, *Direct*, has a high inclusion probability only for the production budget. It is the case that the deals struck between distributors and exhibitors when they are separately owned are different as vertically integrated studios that are keen to get more movies through their theaters at all times because this maximizes returns from ticket sales and ancillary items such as food and drink. When the audiences start to fall, an exhibitor will prefer to end its run and show another new movie that will boost attendance figures again. Exhibitors favor signing short-run contracts for movies, but signing can be avoided if the same studio controls production, distribution, and exhibitions [67].

Table 4 shows the IVBMA posterior estimates of the second-stage regression. As discussed in section 4, we have tested instrumental validity based on a Bayesian approach. As mentioned in Section 4, the validity score represents the probability that the instrument condition is not satisfied. All instruments used in the study are essentially zero, which strongly supports the validity of the instrumentation choices. In the second stage, several variables are essential predictors of opening box office revenues. As expected, the number of opening screens and prerelease advertising are

	IncProb	Mean	SD	Quantile	Conditional	
					Mean	SD
Constant	0.529	−0.284	0.725	(−2.078, 0.989)	−0.525	0.926
Sequels	0.963	0.564	0.203	(0, 0.915)	0.585	0.174
Animation	0.147	−0.001	0.065	(−0.166, 0.163)	−0.001	0.170
R	0.103	0.002	0.041	(−0.071, 0.096)	0.016	0.126
PG-13	0.201	0.034	0.096	(−0.001, 0.345)	0.172	0.149
Action/adventure	0.098	0.002	0.034	(−0.041, 0.097)	0.031	0.104
Comedy	0.142	−0.015	0.056	(−0.205, 0.004)	−0.102	0.116
Drama	0.797	−0.238	0.157	(−0.509, 0)	−0.298	0.113
Horror	0.264	0.051	0.113	(0, 0.383)	0.193	0.143
Sci-Fi	0.150	0.007	0.070	(−0.117, 0.215)	0.054	0.173
Mystery/suspense	0.136	−0.012	0.050	(−0.183, 0.007)	−0.089	0.108
Romance	0.129	0.003	0.052	(−0.104, 0.138)	0.019	0.143
Seasonal index	0.569	−0.446	0.668	(−2.013, 0.445)	−0.781	0.723
Critics review	0.291	0.038	0.216	(−0.371, 0.670)	0.130	0.384
Prerelease advertising	0.918	0.452	0.200	(0, 0.758)	0.492	0.153
Opening screens	1	1.287	0.306	(0.756, 1.963)	1.285	0.306
Production budget	0.120	0.008	0.046	(−0.019, 0.164)	0.071	0.115

Table 4.
IVBMA results (second stage).

significant determinants of opening box office gross with high inclusion probabilities. Though it is difficult to disentangle the causal effect of advertising on sales using data on actual box office receipts, it is consistent with previous findings that prerelease advertising has a positive and statistically significant impact on public awareness of a movie and its box office performance [47, 49, 50, 68]. While Elberse and Eliashberg [52] argue that movie attributes and advertising expenditures mostly influence revenues indirectly through their impact on exhibitors' screen allocations, this result supports a significant direct effect of advertising. The number of opening screens is the most important predictor, with an inclusion probability of one, which is also consistent with previous findings [53, 69, 70]. It seems to be the case that the more screens on which new movies were released, the bigger their initial audiences. The higher the audience for a movie in the opening weekend, the higher would be its audience the following week. While audiences inevitably drop off over time, a movie's cinema run would be longer if it got off to a good start. Considering a typically high correlation between opening screens and prerelease advertising, studios' advertising and distribution approaches may be very similar. Other than these two factors, Sequels and Drama show high inclusion probabilities, which may only reflect the characteristics of successful movies in the sample. Though we initially expected a significant effect of seasonality, it turns out to have a weak influence, though it remains relevant. Production budget has low inclusion probability, and it suggests that a movie's production cost is an indicator of the creative talent involved or the extent to which the movie incorporates expensive special effects or uses elaborate set designs [49], but not a good indicator of success. For about 90 films released in the United States from 2008 to 2012 with budgets of more than $100 million, most of them failed to generate enough revenues at the box office to cover their costs [71]. After all, big budgets do not guarantee success, and the only way to know how audiences react to a movie is to wait until it has been released and moviegoers have had the opportunity to see it.

6. Conclusion

Market response models often use endogenous regressors since marketing activities are nonrandom and reflect the firm's strategic behavior. Thus, ignoring the endogeneity of marketing actions will lead to incorrect estimates of response parameters and, consequently, to biased inferences [4, 58]. While researchers have developed various approaches to dealing with endogeneity, including the control function approach, Gaussian copula, or instrument-free approaches, the IV approach remains the technique of choice when dealing with endogeneity in econometrics and other areas of applied research. Almost invariably, empirical work in economics and marketing will be subject to much uncertainty about model specifications. This may be the consequence of the existence of different theories or different ways in which theories can be implemented in empirical models or other aspects such as assumptions about heterogeneity or independence of the observables [72]. It is important to realize that this uncertainty is an inherent part of the marketing response modeling.

We have proposed a computationally efficient solution to the problem of incorporating model uncertainty into IV estimation. The IVBMA method leverages an existing Gibbs sampler and shows that by nesting model moves inside this framework, model averaging can be performed with minimal additional effort. In contrast to the approximate solution proposed by [16], our method yields a theoretically justified, fully Bayesian procedure. The applied examples show this method's benefit, by enabling additional factors to be entertained by the researcher, which are either incorporated where appropriate or promptly dropped.

The CBF approach is only one manner of incorporating model uncertainty in the framework considered. Two other options would be reversible jump schemes [29, 30] or specify a spike and slab prior [73]. We have chosen our approach because it fits nicely into the Gibbs sampling framework, unlike the reversible jump procedure of Koop et al. [29], and still explicitly incorporates uncertainty at the model level, unlike spike and slab type priors at the variable level. However, additional research is needed to explore the tradeoffs between these alternative methods of incorporating model uncertainty.

One assumption crucial to the Gibbs sampler's functioning is the multivariate normality of the residuals in Eq. (2). Conley et al. [74] discuss a Bayesian approach that allows nonparametric estimation of the distribution of error terms in a set of simultaneous equations using a Dirichlet process mixture (DPM). We note that the IVBMA methodology can readily incorporate the DPM framework by simply replacing the IV kernel distributions of [36] with IVBMA kernel distributions. A nonparametric IVBMA approach based on non-normal errors will be one of the model extensions in the future. Another critical issue is assessing instruments' validity in implementing IV methods. The Bayesian version of the Sargan test that we have proposed serves as a natural starting point for more involved methodologies, including latent factors though many features still need to be investigated on this front compared to other strategies.

IVBMA has the potential to be extended to more complicated likelihood frameworks. The proposed model can be extended to latent constructs in the context of structural equations modeling with latent Gaussian factors and, at the same time, selecting the suitable path model [75]. Survival analysis is another area that can benefit from the IVBMA approach in dealing with multiple endogenous regressors and implementing more flexible hazard specifications beyond the proportional hazard model [76]. Since the entire method uses a Gibbs framework, it can be incorporated in any setting where endogeneity, model uncertainty, and latent normality are present. In particular, the linear specification can be relaxed using semiparametric methods such as splines or more flexible approaches involving Gaussian processes. While the algorithms involved would understandably become more complex, the central concept involving using CBFs to assess model uncertainty would remain pertinent.

Appendix A: determining the CBF calculations

Here we outline the calculation of $pr(\mathcal{D}|M_r, \boldsymbol{\beta}_{-r}, \boldsymbol{K})$. Note that

$$pr(\mathcal{D}|M_r, \boldsymbol{\beta}_{-r}, \boldsymbol{K}) = \int_{\Lambda_{M_r}} pr(\mathcal{D}|\boldsymbol{\beta}_r, \boldsymbol{\beta}_{-r}, \boldsymbol{K}) pr(\boldsymbol{\beta}_r|M_r) d\boldsymbol{\beta}_r.$$

Let $\boldsymbol{U}^{(r)}_{M_r}$ be the submatrix of $\boldsymbol{U}^{(r)}$ associated with the variables in M_r and set $\tilde{\boldsymbol{Y}}_r$ as above. Then

$$\int_{\Lambda_{M_r}} pr(\mathcal{D}|\boldsymbol{\beta}_r, \boldsymbol{\beta}_{-r}, \boldsymbol{K}) pr(\boldsymbol{\beta}_r|M_r) d\boldsymbol{\beta}_r \propto \int_{\Lambda_{M_r}} (2\pi)^{-\frac{|M_r|}{2}} exp\left(-\frac{1}{2}\left[-2\hat{\boldsymbol{\beta}}_{M_r}\boldsymbol{\Omega}_{M_r}\boldsymbol{\beta}_r + \boldsymbol{\beta}_{r'}\boldsymbol{\Omega}_{M_r}\boldsymbol{\beta}_r\right]\right) d\boldsymbol{\beta}_r,$$

where

$$\Omega_{M_r} = K_{rr} \boldsymbol{U}_{M_r}^{(r)'} \boldsymbol{U}_{M_r}^{(r)} + \mathbb{I}_{|M_r|},$$

$$\hat{\boldsymbol{\beta}}_{M_r} = K_{rr} \boldsymbol{\Omega}_{M_r}^{-1} \boldsymbol{U}_{M_r}^{(r)'} \tilde{\boldsymbol{Y}}_r.$$

We can now see that the term in the integral is the canonical form of a Gaussian distribution. Appropriate completion therefore yields

$$pr(\mathcal{D}|M_r, \boldsymbol{\beta}_{-r}, \boldsymbol{K}) \propto |\Omega_{M_r}|^{-1/2} exp\left(-\frac{1}{2}\hat{\boldsymbol{\beta}}_{M_r}{}' \boldsymbol{\Omega}_{M_r} \hat{\boldsymbol{\beta}}_{M_r}\right)$$

Appendix B: Posterior determination in the Poisson Case

Let

$$Y_{i1} \sim \mathcal{P}\left(\boldsymbol{U}_i^{(r)'} \boldsymbol{\beta}_i + \varepsilon_{i1}\right),$$

and for $r > 1$,

$$Y_{ir} = \boldsymbol{U}_i^{(r)'} \boldsymbol{\beta}_r + \varepsilon_{ir},$$

where

$$\boldsymbol{\varepsilon}_i \sim \mathcal{N}\left(0, \boldsymbol{K}^{-1}\right).$$

The MCMC for this model roughly follows the algorithm mentioned above, but with the additional handling of the random effect ε_{i1} and the subsequent updating of $\boldsymbol{\beta}_1$. Note that

$$pr(\varepsilon_{i1}|\cdot) \propto pr\left(Y_i|\boldsymbol{U}_i^{(1)}, \boldsymbol{\beta}_1, \varepsilon_{i1}\right) pr(\varepsilon_{i1}|\boldsymbol{\varepsilon}_i \backslash \varepsilon_{i1}, \boldsymbol{K})$$

where

$$pr(\varepsilon_{i1}|\boldsymbol{\varepsilon}_i \backslash \varepsilon_{i1}, \boldsymbol{K}) = \mathcal{N}\left(\eta_i, \kappa_i^{-1}\right)$$

with

$$\eta_i = -\sum_{r=2}^{R} \frac{K_{1r}}{K_{11}} \varepsilon_{ir}$$

$$\kappa_i = \frac{1}{K_{11}}$$

Further, denote $\mu_i = \boldsymbol{U}_i^{(1)'} \boldsymbol{\beta}_1$. Then

$$pr(\varepsilon_{i1}|\cdot) \propto exp\left(-exp\left(\mu_i + \varepsilon_{i1}\right) + \left(\mu_i + \varepsilon_{i1}\right) Y_{i1}\right) exp\left(-\frac{1}{2}\kappa_i\left(\varepsilon_{i1} - \eta_i\right)^2\right).$$

Writing

$$f(\varepsilon_{i1}) = -exp(\mu_i + \varepsilon_{i1}) + (\mu_i + \varepsilon_{i1})Y_{i1} - \frac{1}{2}\kappa_i(\varepsilon_{i1} - \eta_i)^2$$

we have

$$f'(\varepsilon_{i1}) = -exp(\mu_i + \varepsilon_{i1}) + Y_{i1} - \kappa_i(\varepsilon_{i1} - \eta_i)$$
$$f''(\varepsilon_{i1}) = -exp(\mu_i + \varepsilon_{i1}) - \kappa_i$$

Hence, by setting

$$b(\varepsilon_{i1}) = f'(\varepsilon_{i1}) - f''(\varepsilon_{i1})\varepsilon_{i1}$$
$$c(\varepsilon_{i1}) = -f''(\varepsilon_{i1})$$

we may sample $\varepsilon_{i1}' \sim \mathcal{N}(b(\varepsilon_{i1})/c(\varepsilon_{i1}), 1/c(\varepsilon_{i1}))$ and accept this update with probability $min\{\alpha, 1\}$ where

$$\alpha = \frac{pr(Y_{i1}|\mu_i, \varepsilon_{i1}')pr(\varepsilon_{i1}'|\eta_i, \kappa_i)pr(\varepsilon_{i1}|b(\varepsilon_{i1}'), c(\varepsilon_{i1}'))}{pr(Y_{i1}|\mu_i, \varepsilon_{i1})pr(\varepsilon_{i1}|\eta_i, \kappa_i)pr(\varepsilon_{i1}'|b(\varepsilon_{i1}), c(\varepsilon_{i1}))}.$$

Once all ε_{i1} are updated, other updates mostly follow the steps above.

Author details

Jonathan Lee[1*] and Alex Lenkoski[2]

1 College of Business and Public Management, University of La Verne, La Verne, CA, United States

2 Norwegian Computing Center, Oslo, Norway

*Address all correspondence to: jlee2@laverne.edu

References

[1] Papies D, Ebbes P, Van Heerde HJ. Addressing endogeneity in marketing models. In: Leeflang PSH, Wieringa JE, Bijmolt THA, Pauwels KH, editors. Advanced Methods for Modeling Markets. Cham: Springer International Publishing; 2017. pp. 581-627. DOI: 10.1007/978-3-319-53,469-5_18

[2] Dong X, Chintagunta PK, Manchanda P. A new multivariate count data model to study multi-category physician prescription behavior. Quantitative Marketing and Economics. 2011;**9**: 301-337. DOI: 10.1007/s11129-011-9102-7

[3] Chintagunta P, Erdem T, Rossi PE, Wedel M. Structural modeling in marketing: Review and assessment. Marketing Science. 2006;**25**:604-616. DOI: 10.1287/mksc.1050.0161

[4] Hult GTM, Hair JF, Proksch D, Sarstedt M, Pinkwart A, Ringle CM. Addressing endogeneity in international marketing applications of partial least squares structural equation modeling. Journal of International Marketing. 2018; **26**:1-21. DOI: 10.1509/jim.17.0151

[5] Manchanda P, Rossi PE, Chintagunta PK. Response modeling with nonrandom marketing-mix variables. Journal of Marketing Research. 2004;**41**:467-478. DOI: 10.1509/jmkr.41.4.467.47005

[6] Chintagunta PK. Endogeneity and heterogeneity in a probit demand model: Estimation using aggregate data. Marketing Science. 2001;**20**:442-456. DOI: 10.1287/mksc.20.4.442.9751

[7] Villas-Boas JM, Winer RS. Endogeneity in brand choice models. Management Science. 1999;**45**: 1324-1338. DOI: 10.1287/mnsc.45.10.1324

[8] Rossi PE. Even the rich can make themselves poor: A critical examination of IV methods in marketing applications. Marketing Science. 2014;**33**:655-672. DOI: 10.1287/mksc.2014.0860

[9] Park S, Gupta S. Handling endogenous regressors by joint estimation using copulas. Marketing Science. 2012;**31**:567-586. DOI: 10.1287/mksc.1120.0718

[10] Ebbes P, Papies D, Heerde HJ. The sense and non-sense of holdout sample validation in the presence of endogeneity. Marketing Science. 2011; **30**:1115-1122. DOI: 10.1287/mksc.1110.0666

[11] Kuksov D, Villas-Boas JM. Endogeneity and individual consumer choice. Journal of Marketing Research. 2008;**45**:702-714. DOI: 10.1509/jmkr.45.6.702

[12] Louviere J, Train K, Ben-Akiva M, Bhat C, Brownstone D, Cameron TA, et al. Recent progress on endogeneity in choice modeling. Marketing Letters. 2005;**16**:255-265. DOI: 10.1007/s11002-005-5890-4

[13] Petrin A, Train K. A control function approach to endogeneity in consumer choice models. Journal of Marketing Research. 2010;**47**:3-13. DOI: 10.1509/jmkr.47.1.3

[14] Luan Y, Sudhir K. Forecasting marketing-mix responsiveness for new products. Journal of Marketing Research. 2010;**47**:444-457. DOI: 10.1509/jmkr.47.3.444

[15] Moral-Benito E. Dynamic panels with predetermined regressors: Likelihood-based estimation and

Bayesian averaging with an application to cross-country growth. Banco de Espana Working Paper. 2011. DOI: 10.2139/ssrn.1844186

[16] Lenkoski A, Eicher TS, Raftery AE. Two-stage Bayesian model averaging in endogenous variable models. Econometric Reviews. 2014;**33**:37-41. DOI: 10.1080/07474938.2013.807150

[17] Fernández C, Ley E, Steel MFJ. Benchmark priors for Bayesian model averaging. Journal of Econometrics. 2001;**100**:381-427. DOI: 10.1016/S0304-4076(00)00076-2

[18] Moral-Benito E. Model averaging in economics: An overview. Journal of Economic Surveys. 2015;**29**:46-75. DOI: 10.1111/joes.12044

[19] Abrevaya J, Hausman JA, Khan S. Testing for causal effects in a generalized regression model with endogenous regressors. Econometrica. 2010;**78**: 2043-2061. DOI: 10.3982/ecta7133

[20] Lewis SM, Eccleston JA, Russell KG. Designs for generalized linear models with several variables and model uncertainty. Technometrics. 2006;**48**:284-292. DOI: 10.1198/004017005000000571

[21] Clyde M, George EI. Model uncertainty. Statistical Science. 2004;**19**: 81-94. DOI: 10.1214/088342304000000035

[22] Raftery A. Approximate Bayes factors and accounting for model uncertainty in generalized linear models. Biometrika. 1996;**83**:251-266. DOI: 10.1093/biomet/83.2.251

[23] Hinne M, Gronau QF, van den Bergh D, Wagenmakers E-J. A conceptual introduction to Bayesian model averaging. Advances in Methods and Practices in Psychological Science. 2020; **3**(2):200-215. DOI: 10.1177/2515245919898657

[24] Cohen-Cole E, Durlauf S, Fagan J, Nagin D. Model uncertainty and the deterrent effect of capital punishment. American Law and Economics Review. 2009;**11**:335-369. DOI: 10.1093/aler/ahn001

[25] Durlauf SN, Kourtellos A, Tan CM. Is god in the details? A reexamination of the role of religion in economic growth. Journal of Applied Econometrics. 2012; **27**:1059-1075. DOI: 10.1002/jae.1245

[26] Kleibergen F, Zivot E. Bayesian and classical approaches to instrumental variable regression. Journal of Econometrics. 2003;**114**:29-72. DOI: 10.1016/S0304-4076(02)00219-1

[27] Kass RE, Wasserman L. A reference test for nested hypotheses with large samples. Journal of the American Statistical Association. 1995;**90**:928-934. DOI: 10.1080/01621459.1995.10476592

[28] Mirestean AT, Tsangarides CG, Chen H. Limited information Bayesian model averaging for dynamic panels with short time periods. IMF Working Papers. 2009;**2009**:A001. DOI: 10.5089/9781451872217.001

[29] Koop G, Leon-Gonzalez R, Strachan R. Bayesian model averaging in the instrumental variable regression model. Journal of Econometrics. 2012;**171**: 237-250. DOI: 10.1016/j.jeconom.2012.06.005

[30] Green PJ. Reversible jump Markov Chain Monte Carlo computation and Bayesian model determination. Biometrika. 1995;**82**:711-732. DOI: 10.1093/biomet/82.4.711

[31] Holmes CC, Denison DGT, Mallick BK. Accounting for model uncertainty in

seemingly unrelated regressions. Journal of Computational and Graphical Statistics. 2002;**11**:533-551. DOI: 10.1198/106186002475

[32] Drèze JH. Bayesian limited information analysis of the simultaneous equations model. Econometrica. 1976; **44**:1045-1075. DOI: 10.2307/1911544

[33] Kleibergen F, van Dijk HK. Bayesian simultaneous equations analysis using reduced rank structures. Econometric Theory. 1998;**14**:701-743. DOI: 10.1017/S0266466698146017

[34] Strachan R, Inder B. Bayesian analysis of the error correction model. Journal of Econometrics. 2004;**123**:307-325. DOI: 10.1016/j.jeconom.2003.12.004

[35] Madigan D, York J. Bayesian graphical models for discrete data. International Statistical Review. 1995;**63**: 215-232. DOI: 10.2307/1403615

[36] Rossi PE, Allenby GM, McCulloch R. Bayesian Statistics and Marketing. New York: Wiley; 2006. DOI: 10.1002/0470863692

[37] Dickey JM, Gunel E. Bayes factors from mixed probabilities. Journal of the Royal Statistical Society: Series B: Methodological. 1978;**40**:43-46. DOI: 10.1111/j.2517-6161.1978.tb01645.x

[38] Sargan JD. The estimation of economic relationships with instrumental variables. Econometrica. 1958;**26**:393-415. DOI: 10.2307/1907619

[39] McCulloch CE, Searle S, Neuhaus JM. Generalized, Linear, and Mixed Models. 2nd ed. Hoboken, NJ: John Wiley & Sons, Inc.; 2008

[40] Natarajan R, Kass RE. Reference Bayesian methods for generalized linear mixed models. Journal of the American Statistical Association. 2000;**95**:227-237. DOI: 10.1080/01621459.2000.10473916

[41] Zeger SL, Karim MR. Generalized linear models with random effects: A Gibbs sampling approach. Journal of the American Statistical Association. 1991; **86**:79-86. DOI: 10.2307/2289717

[42] McCulloch CE, Nelder JA. Generalized Linear Models. 2nd ed. Chapman and Hall; 1989

[43] van Ravenzwaaij D, Cassey P, Brown SD. A simple introduction to Markov Chain Monte–Carlo sampling. Psychological Bulletin & Review. 2018; **25**:143-154. DOI: 10.3758/s13423-016-1015-8

[44] Hall DB. Zero-inflated Poisson and binomial regression with random effects: A case study. Biometrics. 2000;**56**:1030-1039. DOI: 10.1111/j.0006-341X.2000.01030.x

[45] Albert J. A Bayesian analysis of a Poisson random effects model for home run hitters. The American Statistician. 1992;**46**:246-253. DOI: 10.2307/2685306

[46] Kass RE, Raftery AE. Bayes factors. Journal of the American Statistical Association. 1995;**90**:773-795. DOI: 10.1080/01621459.1995.10476572

[47] Gunter B. Predicting Movie Success at the Box Office. Palgrave Macmillan Cham: Springer International Publishing; 2018

[48] Rao VR, Ravid SAA, Gretz RT, Chen J, Basuroy S. The impact of advertising content on movie revenues. Marketing Letters. 2017;**28**:341-355. DOI: 10.1007/s11002-017-9418-5

[49] Elberse A, Anand B. The effectiveness of pre-release advertising for motion pictures: An empirical

investigation using a simulated market. Information Economics and Policy. 2007;**19**:319-343. DOI: 10.1016/j.infoecopol.2007.06.003

[50] Zufryden FS. Linking advertising to box office performance of new film releases - a marketing planning model. Journal of Advertising Research. 1996; **36**:29

[51] Joshi A, Hanssens DM. The direct and indirect effects of advertising spending on firm value. Journal of Marketing. 2010;**74**:20-33. DOI: 10.1509/jmkg.74.1.20

[52] Elberse A, Eliashberg J. Demand and supply dynamics for sequentially released products in international markets: The case of motion pictures. Marketing Science. 2003;**22**:329-354. DOI: 10.1287/mksc.22.3.329.17740

[53] Neelamegham R, Chintagunta PK. A Bayesian model to forecast new product performance in domestic and international markets. Marketing Science. 1999;**18**:115-136. DOI: 10.1287/mksc.18.2.115

[54] Chang BH, Ki EJ. Devising a practical model for predicting theatrical movie success: Focusing on the experience good property. Journal of Media Economics. 2005;**18**:247-269. DOI: 10.1207/s15327736me1804_2

[55] Basuroy S, Chatterjee S, Ravid SA. How critical are critical reviews? The box office effects of film critics, star power, and budgets. Journal of Marketing. 2003; **67**:103-117. DOI: 10.1509/jmkg.67.4.103.18692

[56] Wasserman M, Mukherjee S, Scott K, Zeng XHT, Radicchi F, Amaral LAN. Correlations between user voting data, budget, and box office for films in the internet movie database. Journal of the Association for Information Science and Technology. 2015;**66**:858-868. DOI: 10.1002/asi.23213

[57] Simonton DK. Cinematic creativity and production budgets: Does money make the movie? The Journal of Creative Behavior. 2005;**39**:1-15. DOI: 10.1002/j.2162-6057.2005.tb01246.x

[58] Dong X, Manchanda P, Chintagunta P. Quantifying the benefits of individual-level targeting in the presence of firm strategic behavior. Journal of Marketing Research. 2009;**46**:207-221. DOI: 10.1509/jmkr.46.2.207

[59] Sood S, Drze X. Brand extensions of experiential goods: Movie sequel evaluations. Journal of Consumer Research. 2006;**33**:352-360. DOI: 10.1086/508520

[60] Basuroy S, Chatterjee S. Fast and frequent: Investigating box office revenues of motion picture sequels. Journal of Business Research. 2008;**61**: 798-803. DOI: 10.1016/j.jbusres.2007.07.030

[61] Smith D, Park C. The effects of brand extensions on market share and advertising efficiency. Journal of Marketing Research. 1992;**29**(3):296-313. DOI: 10.2307/3172741

[62] Ravid SA. Information, blockbusters and stars? A study of the film industry. The Journal of Business. 1999;**72**:463-492. DOI: 10.1086/209624

[63] Joshi M, Das D, Gimpel K, Smith NA. Movie reviews and revenues: An experiment in text regression. Human Language Technologies: The 2010 Annual Conference of the North American Chapter of the Association for Computational Linguistics, USA: Association for Computational Linguistics: 2010, p. 293–296.

[64] Debenedetti S, Ghariani G. To quote or not to quote? Critics' quotations in film advertisements as indicators of the continuing authority of film criticism. Poetics. 2018;**66**:30-41. DOI: 10.1016/j.poetic.2018.02.003

[65] Reinstein D, Snyder MC. The influence of expert reviews on consumer demand for experience goods: A case study of movie critics. Journal of Industrial Economics. 2005;**53**:27-51. DOI: 10.1111/j.0022-1821.2005.00244.x

[66] Legoux R, Larocque D, Laporte S, Belmati S, Boquet T. The effect of critical reviews on exhibitors' decisions: Do reviews affect the survival of a movie on screen? International Journal of Research in Marketing. 2016;**33**:357-374. DOI: 10.1016/j.ijresmar.2015.07.003

[67] Filson D, Switzer D, Besocke P. At the movies: The economics of exhibition contracts. Economic Inquiry. 2005;**43**:354-369. DOI: 10.1093/ei/cbi024

[68] Eliashberg J, Jonker JJ, Sawhney MS, Wierenga B. MOVIEMOD: An implementable decision-support system for prerelease market evaluation of motion pictures. Marketing Science. 2000;**19**:226-243. DOI: 10.1287/mksc.19.3.226.11796

[69] Rao A, Hartmann W. Quality vs. variety: Trading larger screens for more shows in the era of digital cinema. Quantitative Marketing and Economics. 2015;**13**:117-134. DOI: 10.1007/s11129-015-9156-z

[70] Moul CC, Shugan SM. Theatrical release and the launching of motion pictures. In: Moul CC, editor. A Concise Handbook of Movie Industry Economics. Cambridge: Cambridge University Press; 2005. pp. 80-137. DOI: 10.1017/CBO9780511614422.005

[71] Ghiassi M, Lio D, Moon B. Pre-production forecasting of movie revenues with a dynamic artificial neural network. Expert Systems with Applications. 2015;**42**:3176-3193. DOI: 10.1016/j.eswa.2014.11.022

[72] Steel MFJ. Model averaging and its use in economics. Journal of Economic Literature. 2020;**58**:644-719. DOI: 10.1257/jel.20191385

[73] George EI, McCulloch RE. Variable selection via Gibbs sampling. Journal of the American Statistical Association. 1993;**88**:881-889. DOI: 10.1080/01621459.1993.10476353

[74] Conley TG, Hansen CB, McCulloch RE, Rossi PE. A semi-parametric Bayesian approach to the instrumental variable problem. Journal of Econometrics. 2008;**144**:276-305. DOI: 10.1016/j.jeconom.2008.01.007

[75] Kaplan D, Lee C. Bayesian model averaging over directed acyclic graphs with implications for the predictive performance of structural equation models. Structural Equation Modeling: A Multidisciplinary Journal. 2016;**23**:343-353. DOI: 10.1080/10705511.2015.1092088

[76] Volinsky CT, Madigan D, Raftery AE, Kronmal RA. Bayesian model averaging in proportional hazard models: Assessing the risk of a stroke. Journal of the Royal Statistical Society: Series C: Applied Statistics. 1997;**46**:433-448. DOI: 10.1111/1467-9876.00082